ALEX DIAZ, SHACKED, EL FRONTON, GRAN CANARIA. DANI HERNANDEZ

THE
BODYBOARD
TRAVEL GUIDE

WHERE TO SCORE THE WORLD'S BEST BODYBOARDING WAVES

The Bodyboard Travel Guide
Owen Pye with Rob Barber and Mike Searle

Published by Orca Publications
Berry Road Studios
Berry Road
Newquay
Cornwall
TR7 1AT
United Kingdom
(+44) 01637 878074
www.threesixtymag.co.uk
www.orcasurf.co.uk

EDITOR: **ROB BARBER**
PROJECT DIRECTOR: **MIKE SEARLE**
DESIGNER: **DAVID ALCOCK**
DISTRIBUTION CONSULTANT: **CHRIS POWER**

PHOTOGRAPHERS: Mike Searle, Chris Power, Roger Sharp, Alan Van Gysen, Alex
Williams, Sacha Specker, Ray Collins, Tim McKenna, Chris Van Lennep, Owen Pye,
David Alcock, Will Bailey, Kirstin Prisk, Clare McGowan, Lucia Griggi, Rob Hazelwood,
Roke/Basterretxea, Jakue Anditokoetxea, Gary Knights, Sebastien Bigot, James
Bowden, Jason Feast, Seamus Makim, Dani Hernandez, Reda Wave Hunter, Ricardo
Borghi, Dale Adams, Simon Heale, Victor Gonzales Garcia, Alex Wells, Kate Czuczman,
Piping, Nate Lawrence, InwaterBali, Jason Reposar, Chris Burt, John Callahan, Chis
Gurney, Tim Jones, Lee Kelly, Paul Castle, Simon Williams, Joli, Todd Glaser, Josh
Tabone, Rod Owen, David P'uu, Scott Winer, Jeff Flindt, Jason Kubell, Jimmy Johnson,
Andrew Rams, IBA/Catalano, Tungsten, David Baker, Shea Sevilla, Pete Gleeson,
Fernando Munoz, Stu Norton, Kris Inch, Edwin Morales, Ben DeCamp

SPECIAL THANKS TO THE FOLLOWING EDITORIAL CONTRIBUTORS: Ryan Hardy, Jared
Houston, Ben Player, Mark McCarthy, Michael Novy, Mathieu Desaphie, Pablo Prieto,
Pierre Louis Costes, Toze Fonseca, Sacha Specker, Damian Prisk, Alex Uranga, Jason
Finlay, Matt Lackey, Jeff Hubbard, Jake Stone, Dave Winchester, Dallas Singer, Damian
King, Jacob Romero, Mike Stewart, Amaury Lavernhe, Magno Oliveira, Michelle Rozzen

ISBN: 978-0-9567893-0-3

PRINTED AND BOUND: **GREAT WALL PRINTING, HONG KONG**

On the cover: Tom Gillespie, in the pit at Riley's in Ireland. Photo: Mickey Smith.
This page: Dawn surf check for Aidan Salmon and Rob Barber in Nicaragua. Photo: Sharpy.

CONTENTS

SHAUN PYNE TRAVELLED HALFWAY AROUND
THE WORLD FROM AUSTRALIA TO IRELAND
TO SCORE THIS GOLD.

MICKEY SMITH

INTRODUCTION

"The world is a book, and those who don't travel are only reading one page." – *ST. AUGUSTINE*

Travel. As bodyboarders it drives us, inspires us, and defines who we are. Wandering nomads. Squinting at the horizon, boards under our arms, dried salt in the creases of our foreheads. How many of us have spent time on Google Earth scanning the coastline of some distant location looking for wrapping swell lines and possible setups? The search for the perfect bodyboarding wave is instilled in us, be it in hitchhiking from one cove to the next at home, or cruising from one island to the next on an expensive Pacific boat trip.

I know, I know, having had a quick flick through the contents already you can't believe Spot X hasn't made the cut. I can almost hear you now: "Eh?! Why has that break been chosen when Spot X hasn't been?!" In truth there are ten thousand spot X's which could have made the pages of this book, but you have to draw the line somewhere. Every one of the 100 spots in this book has been handpicked due to its ability to dish out perfect bodyboarding waves. From epic wedges, dredging slabs, peeling beachies, heavy shories, firing rivermouths, reeling points to hollow reefs, I hope this book will inspire you to look beyond the horizon and start planning your next trip.

To travel is to enrich your existence, to open your mind to ways of life far removed from your own, to put your problems into perspective and make you appreciate the rest of the world outside of your little bubble. Among everything you experience when you travel, from the colourful cultures and traditions of distant lands to the flamboyant food and people, the one thing that really gets the heart pounding is the search for waves. All of these spots are less than 24 hours from you, so stop hiding behind your excuses and get involved. It only stays a dream if you let it.

– *Owen Pye*

FOREWORD

By Mitch Rawlins

EVER SINCE I WAS A YOUNG GROM I WAS
ALWAYS EXPLORING, LOOKING OUT AT
THE OCEAN OR TO THE NEXT RIDGE OF A
MOUNTAIN. IT FELT NATURAL TO ME TO
WANT GO AFTER THE UNKNOWN, TO WANT TO
FIND OUT WHAT WAS AHEAD.

Later on in life, bodyboarding and travelling
allowed me to further explore this liquid earth and
the many waves it has to offer. From your local
break to the other side of the world, wherever there
is a coast there are waves and waves and more
waves. Around the next bay, who knows, there
could be a Kirra right there for all I know.

Curiosity is an amazing thing, it's led me to
some amazing experiences out in the ocean and on
land. Curiosity also allows you to interact with the
environment you are in.

Take for example the slabs people are riding
these days. Bodyboarders are curious to find out
what is ridable and what is not and we are travelling
to great lengths to find these new off-the-grid
places.

My advice to anyone travelling looking for waves
is to stay curious and never let a long walk get in the
way of a new discovery.

—*Mitch Rawlins*

PLANNING YOUR TRIP

By Owen Pye

While the peak swell season will virtually guarantee waves in many destinations, so the rest of the world will be eyeing up the charts alongside you, ready to pounce on the same cheap flights and camps to share the same lineup of 100 dudes. It can sometimes pay to gamble on the off-season; while sick waves aren't guaranteed and the seasonal trades may not be ideal, you are almost assured a lack of crowds and on the days it does turn on you'll be seriously stoked it paid off.

It could be worth jotting down your aims and get the basics of your trip nailed to accommodate them. If you really want to surf a couple of specific spots and you don't mind waiting in a hideous pack to get that one barrel you've always dreamed of, then hitting it peak season is probably your best bet. Conversely, if you hate crowds and don't mind searching a bit in unfavourable weather to find a sick setup facing the other way which only ever works on reverse trades, then the off-season could be the winning ticket instead.

Flights and accommodation will almost always be cheaper outside of holiday periods and peak times. If you can get some time off and book your trip with off-season flights you should hopefully be able to find discounted rates on renting a pad when you get there too. You'll often find the earlier you book the cheaper they'll be, but it is possible to get some insane last minute bargains. While stories of guys rocking up at an airport with boog bags and asking over the counter for the next flight to anywhere have occasionally worked spectacularly well, by leaving it late you run the risk of limited choice and a higher price if nothing can be found.

If you are flying on a budget it might be worth looking into the countries whose peak swell season coincides with their off-season tourist industry to blag the best prices. Ticking the box of both is sure to yield some great waves without breaking the bank.

When it comes to planning your trip, things of course vary greatly depending on whom you are thinking of going with — if anyone. Flying solo has major advantages; you hardly ever get hassle from locals as you aren't one of a mobile rent-a-crowd, you don't have to make compromises for the good of the group, you meet far more people, and are free to take off on impromptu random tangents and boat trips which will inevitably crop up once you are out there.

If you plan on going with others, the first thing to do is be absolutely certain you will get on well with them – travelling, bodyboarding and living with the same person 24 hours a day can quickly deteriorate if you aren't careful, especially if they have a penchant of getting dangerously disrespectful when drunk. The last thing you want is to get embroiled with a dozen local heavies because your pissed loudmouth mate tried it on with the wrong girl. A little foresight to your travelling companions

TIM MCKENNA

goes a long way!

If you are going in a group, talk about what you want to achieve on the trip, be it certain spots, specific islands or particular cultural highlights. Do your research and see what else might interest you as a group nearby in case it goes flat ... while insane swell consistency is championed by all the surf camp websites, you can't rule out mother nature just not playing ball during your stay. Having backup activities is always a good thing, although you'll probably come across a few whilst you're out there too. I didn't know the sport of horseboarding existed for example until I once had a chance beach encounter with a horse bound Fijian carrying a length of rope and an old surfboard. (I wasn't very good).

If you have mates at home who have travelled to certain places before, tap them up for info on spots, accommodation and most importantly any locals they're still in contact with and wouldn't mind hooking you up with. One of the beauties of travelling is meeting people and making friends all over the globe. Do enough of it and you'll never have to pay for a room on a trip again ... leaving countries with new friends who'll welcome you back is both incredibly useful and a privilege. Having local knowledge of an area is unbeatable, and being able to bro-down with a local crew could be the golden key to your trip.

WHEN?
WHERE?
WHY?

The best destinations for:

For the first-timer: California, France, Portugal, Bali, England

For the intermediate bodyboarder: Australia (East Coast), Indo, Brazil.

For the hardcore charger: Ireland, Tahiti, Scotland, Hawaii, Mexico, Canaries, Indo, Pacific Islands, Australia (WA).

Escaping the Northern Hemisphere winter: Morocco, Canaries, Hawaii, South Africa. Mexico, Central America, Chile, Caribbean.

Escaping the Southern Hemi winter: Bali, Philippines, Central America,

Most consistent: Central America, Pacific Islands, South Africa

Best from December to February: Hawaii, Canaries, Morocco, California.

Best from March to May: Portugal, Spain, Australia, Indo.

Best from June to August: Australia, Indo, Central America

Best from September to November: France, Portugal, Spain, East Coast USA, Ireland, Scotland, England.

Best for year-round consistency: Chile, Mexico.

Heaviest vibe in the water: Hawaii, Tahiti, Canary Islands

Most laid back vibe: Brazil, Morocco, Philippines, Pacific Islands, Ireland, Caribbean

Best places to avoid sharks and other wildlife: UK, France, Spain, Portugal, North East Coast USA.

Best surfing destinations for culture: Spain, Portugal, England, Morocco, Indo.

Best for desert experiences: Chile, Morocco, Western Australia.

Best for nightlife: Brazil, Cornwall (July and August), Gold Coast, New York.

Best for the adventurous explorer: Philippines, Indo (away from Bali), Ireland, Scotland, Pacific Islands, Australia, South Africa.

Least crowded: Scotland, Ireland, Philippines (away from Cloud 9), Pacific Islands.

THE KIND OF VIEW THAT MAKES HOURS OF SITTING ON A
PLANE WORTHWHILE. NORTH BEACH, DURBAN.

SHOOTING YOUR TRIP

By Mike Searle

You go on a bodyboarding trip to score the waves of your life, so you will also want to keep some photos to capture those memories and for bragging to your mates back home about all the epic barrels and huge airs you had. Don't fill your Facebook page with hundreds of boring blurry images, follow these quick tips to get some stunners.

EQUIPMENT

Photographers too often get obsessed with spending big bucks on the latest gear, but don't forget it's the human being taking the picture, not the camera. You *can* get good shots with a smartphone, but you'll get even better shots if you invest in a decent compact. Go

for one with a lens that has a decent wide angle (look for 28mm equivalent) and zoom for some close-up action.

If your budget stretches and you want to get some better quality images without having to lug around a bulky DSLR, go for one of the compact system cameras with interchangeable lenses, like the Olympus PEN series.

If you are into your photography and have or are considering buying a DSLR, make sure you have enough cash left over for a couple of good lenses and a tripod. While most DSLRs come with a decent enough 18-55mm lens or equivalent, it might be worth splashing out for an ultra wide angle (in the region of 10-20mm) for lifestyle shots, and telephoto (50-250mm or longer)

for zoomed-in action shots from the beach. You can also get great portraits with a telephoto, keeping your subjects sharp and blurring the background, known as depth of field.

If it is new, play around at home and learn your way around the body of the camera so you'll know it inside out and won't miss a thing when you are out there and the perfect shot pops up.

CHOOSE YOUR LIGHT

Photographers call the hour or so after dawn and before dusk the 'golden hours'. This is the best light for outdoor shots with golden glows and surreal sky colours. By about midday until late afternoon the sun is just too harsh to get pleasing results. Avoid cloudy days too, no point in taking shots when it's gloomy.

CREATE AN IMAGE

The difference between the pros and everyone else is that they 'create an image' rather than just take a shot of what's there. Look around for rocks, trees, or a shack on the beach, a boat on the horizon or pretty girl walking by and try and incorporate them in the shot. Framing a peeling lineup with some palm trees may be an old trick, but it's a good one.

WORK THE ANGLES

Move around and look for a more striking angle. See how the light changes as you change position. Get low, or see what happens when you shoot from a high viewpoint. Photography is a creative art, so use your imagination. Think of your holiday album as a portfolio, so mix it up to get some good variety. Modern digital compacts also have amazing macro settings (usually shown on the control dial as a flower) which mean you can get in really close and shoot the details like flowers, insects and textures. Don't go mad but this is the kind of stuff that most people miss.

COMPOSE

There are a few laws of composition which will help you snap more pleasing shots. The most widely used one is the 'rule of thirds'. If you divide the image into

thirds with two imaginary vertical and two horizontal lines, important elements in the image should roughly be placed along those lines and at their intersections. Slightly off-centre subjects work much better than centred ones, and horizons should normally never divide the image in half. Or be a little wonky, schoolboy error!

PEOPLE

When travelling in a strange land keep an eye out for interesting looking people to photograph. Smile and ask them politely if you can take their photo. If you don't speak their language pointing to the camera is normally a good move. In poor countries it helps to have a pocketful of change to help the transaction along. Frame your photograph, and then get closer. Most people stand too far back and don't fill the frame, especially if you're shooting the grizzled face of a gnarly Indo dude with one tooth.

GOPRO

If you want to shoot HD video then a GoPro is the best bet for in-the-tube point of view shots. Practice with it before you go so you know where the best place is to fix it. While it might initially seem rad to have it pointing up at your scraggly little beard, most people are more keen to mindsurf

the forward shot of the barrel itself, maybe framed with your arms or torso if you can mount it near a rail. Get creative, try different mounts and rigs, and mix it up from session to session — the GoPro is by far one of the best investments you can make if you are after some good quality footage of your trip.

BACK UP

Finally, don't forget to download the images onto your netbook or laptop as soon as you get in. There's nothing worse than losing a card full of memories, trust me!

GADGETS

IF YOU'VE GOT SPARE CASH, SPLASH OUT ON SOME OF THESE.

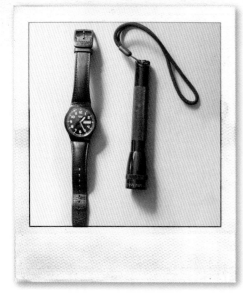

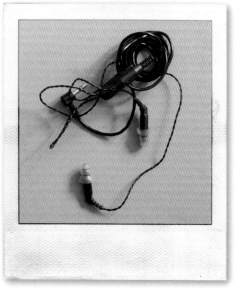

MINI MAGLITE LED FLASHLIGHT

It doesn't matter whether you are trying to find your tent at night or signalling SOS for help, the Mini Maglite LED Flashlight is a life-saver. Not just any old torch, it features two different power settings: a maximum-power setting that yields full brightness, and a 25 per cent power setting to conserve battery power for reading at night, or for a prolonged emergency. It's also worth buying flashlight that fits on your head like a miner's lamp.

WATERPROOF WATCH

Always worth getting a decent, hard-wearing, waterproof watch to keep you on track for flights, trains, buses or anything else you have to catch. On top of which it is invaluable for quick surfs when you are on a timer and can't afford to be late for something. Can also be used to try and bribe border officials when your passport has expired and you have reached a sweaty, panicked desperation.

BUSHNELL H2O 8X25 BINOCULARS

Very useful for frontier and boat trips to spot waves breaking off far away fringe reefs, the compact Bushnell H2O 8x25 binoculars will give you eight-times magnification to suddenly transform a distant remote reef pass flick of water into the glory of a full-frame barrelling wonder, ready for plunder.

6.5W GLOBAL SOLAR SUNLINQ E-SUN PORTABLE FOLDING SOLAR PANEL

This waterproof and portable solar panel folds up nice and small but boasts near universal connectivity;
able to charge
all your
handheld
devices
(like your
smartphone,

mp3 player, camera, etc), rechargeable batteries, other small 12v accessories, and is even powerful enough to recharge a 12v vehicle battery should you find yourself unable to start your car in the middle of nowhere

ETYMOTIC RESEARCH ER-4P NOISE-CANCELLING PORTABLE EARPHONES

One of the world's best single-driver earphones, the Etymotic Research ER-4P's are an absolute necessity for any long-haul flight or for audiophiles who crave top-end sound quality on the go. The triple-flange and foam-tip buds of the earphones passively block out up to 41dB of ambient sound (perfect for planes, ferries or buses) allowing you to completely silence the screaming baby on the row in front and listen to your music naturally at safe volume levels. The lightweight and comfortable earphones are considered the next-best thing to live music with superb and unrivalled natural sound, allowing you to hear the full dynamic range of recordings, just as the band intended.

These earphones slay anything you were previously considering, unless you were remortgaging your house for the custom-moulded monitors of Ultimate Ears.

THE LEATHERMAN WAVE MULTI TOOL

The ultimate companion for any trip, the Leatherman Wave Multi Tool features 17 tools all in one compact pocket-friendly design. Whether you are under the bonnet of an overheating Toyota Land Cruiser or deep in a Fijian jungle cutting down vines to lash together a raft, the Leatherman has your back.

ALOKSAK WATERPROOF BAGS

If the US Navy have tested and approved them, we can pretty much vouch for their quality – the

ultimate super lightweight bags for keeping your stuff dry, be it from an impromptu tropical downpour or freediving beyond 200ft. Ideal for your phone, passport, map, clothing, food, batteries, netbook, cables, electrical gear ... the bag has been cold-rated to -40C and hermetically seals via a Ziploc making it completely water and dustproof. Sorted.

NETBOOK, $320 +

The lightweight, portable and inexpensive netbook is perfect for travelling, taking up minimal space in your bag and providing good battery life. Most sport screens smaller than 12" and come with built-in webcams and wireless, so these little machines take care of all your needs: internet browsing, emailing, blogging, writing, photo editing, Skyping, storing your photos and videos, watching films, you name it. Netbooks are the perfect little laptop for sorting out your life when on the road.

SMARTPHONE, $FREE ON SOME PHONE CONTRACTS

Smartphones have quickly become an indispensible piece of kit such is the speed and advancement of mobile technology in recent years. Not only are many phones tri or quad-band, facilitating use abroad, but almost all are internet and email-enabled so you are always hooked up. Add to this their massive storage of up to 32gb for thousands of songs and movies they also now pack high-quality HD cameras, for shooting or recording the hilarious mishaps that will no doubt happen on your trip. They are, simply put, the most versatile handheld device you can get. Oh, did we mention they can be solar-charged too?

AIRPORTS

By Rob Barber

There's no two ways about it, you can make the experience of using an airport almost totally stress-free, all you need is to be prepared, organised and punctual. If you get a decent seat, a couple of films and a bit of sleep, flying can almost be relaxing! Try to think of it as a few hours to dream about the waves that you're about to score, or a table-service reflection on the amazing sessions you've just enjoyed.

HERE ARE SOME WAYS YOU CAN MAKE IT ALL RUN AS SMOOTHLY AS POSSIBLE…

• Be early. Aim to be at the airport at least three hours before your international flight is due to depart. The finer you cut it the more stressed you'll be, and the more you'll be cursing yourself that you've left yourself a two mile sprint to get to gate 366 before your name is called out and the thing starts reversing.

• Check the weight and dimensions of your luggage at home to make sure they fall within your airline's limitations. Budget airlines will generally pick up on this.

• Double-check your carry-on luggage before you pack it, and make sure to remove any sharp objects, liquids, drug paraphernalia, seeds, or anything else that could potentially get you in trouble at the airport. The last thing you want is an aggressive Alsatian stuffing his nose in your gooch and/or the security team finding a big dildo in your bag courtesy of your hilarious mates.

• You'll no doubt have to remove your shoes in the airport a couple of times and your feet will swell up in the air (especially on long-haul flights), so consider choosing slip-ons rather than lace-ups. If you're going to take your shoes off mid flight, make sure that you have new hole-less socks that won't stink up the cabin.

• Get a neck pillow. You'll look like a geek with it wrapped around you but it should save you getting a stiff neck and it will vastly add to your comfort. Plus it will stop your head lolling around and you dribbling over fellow passengers.

• Noise cancelling head or ear phones can be expensive but are worth every last penny to get some head space during a screaming-baby-and-kid-filled flight.

• Enroll in every frequent-flyer programme that you can. A lot of airlines are partnered so your airmiles will be transferable for upgrades, specials etc… bonus.

• Executive lounges are worth the money if you have a long delay. They usually have free wi-fi, free food, drinks and comfortable sofas with TVs. If it costs $30 to get in there work out how much you are likely to spend on food and bits during your seven hour delay and it will probably still be worth splashing out to live the high life.

• If you're not down with prescription drugs to calm your aviophobia, go to a health food shop and buy some Pharma Kava for stress or anxiety and some melatonin for sleeping. These healthy alternatives can make a sketchy flight bearable for any health-conscious white-knuckle flyer. Valium or Ambien can also be prescribed by doctors — you could sleep through a vertical loop the loop on that stuff.

• Consider using the self-service consoles to check in at airports, they will save you stacks of time and are actually surprisingly easy to operate.

• Keep your passport, e-ticket and necessary documents all quick to hand — it saves untold zipping, unzipping and having to constantly take your backpack off to find them.

• Make sure you have your laptop and electronic items stored near the top of your bag so you can whip them out for the X-ray machine without having to dig to the bottom and hold a bunch of people up.

• Remember your manners at the check-in desk. They are used to dealing with complaining fools all day long, so smile, be nice, crack a gag. It could save you the extra baggage cost or even get you an upgrade.

MIKE SEARLE

MIKE SEARLE

PRO TOP TIPS:

RYAN HARDY: "If you have a packing list to tick off and you get to the airport with plenty of time, you can't go wrong."

JARED HOUSTON: "Some airports in the world are now 'Silent Airports' which means they don't announce boarding calls, so my number one tip is to pay attention!"

BEN PLAYER: "Always keep your stuff close and pay attention to it. There's a heap of bad people that prey on people that aren't aware. I once saw someone put their personal belongings through the X-ray machine but got held up with the body scanner. When they got through to the other side all of their stuff had been stolen, the person in front must have picked it all up and got on their flight with the bullion."

OWEN MAKES USE OF THE AIRPORT WIFI.

BUDGET TIPS

By Rob Barber

There is a difference between being a penny-pinching shoestring student and an experienced traveller that is trying to see their budget get them as many waves as possible. Check out the following stealth tips on how to do it the right way.

• When checking in at the airport, keep your board bag as far away from the counter as possible and refer to it as a 'boogieboard'. Most airlines will try to charge you per board and if you don't convince them there is only one board in the bag they will sting you. By using the word 'boogieboard' they tend to

CAMPING OFFERS THE FLEXIBILITY TO KEEP ON THE MOVE, WHILE NOT DAMAGING YOUR TRAVEL FUNDS.

LIVING OUT THE BACK OF A VAN CAN ADD TO THE ADVENTURE AND SAVE YOU VALUABLE $$$.

be less suspicious. If you say it's your 'bodyboard' they are more likely to ask exactly what that is and start ripping the zips open on your bag to find out.

• If you go to sleep in an airport terminal or bus station, keep your zips padlocked and lash your bags to your body so you don't get ripped off. Use your leash!

• Always travel with a well-stocked medical kit. Buy one in advance or get the contents online before you depart or you run the risk of getting fleeced at airport chemists otherwise. If you can perform basic first aid too you could save on extortionate medical bills in foreign countries, so get swotting.

• Carry some surf stickers or US dollar bills to use as currency with the young locals, they are great to trade for local wood carvings or even (sealed!) bottles of water. Tee shirts aren't bad currency either as long as they are in okay condition.

• Carrying your own small travel pillow can make some of the lower budget accommodation options way more tempting. Plus it could save you catching head lice, fleas or a mystery rash.

• Pack a compact, waterproof, LED Headlamp, and load it up with lithium batteries for longer life and better performance in cold weather. These things are great for power cuts, night emergencies or reading your book in a dimly-lit dorm room in a backpackers.

• Get tipping correct. Even if you are on a budget, you won't get far if you skimp on giving correct tips to the locals. Ask a well-versed local what the protocol is and get it right. If you can't afford to tip, don't use the service.

• Don't use your mobile phone abroad; you will have a monster of a bill waiting for you when you get home, especially if it has a tendency to somehow find itself online. I know someone who fell asleep one night with his mobile accidently connected to the internet for 11 hours until morning time. Ouch. Make sure that your phone is unlocked so that you can buy a local SIM card and use that for the duration of your trip.

• If you're staying in a hotel, always lock your valuables, especially your passport, in a safety deposit box if there is one. If there isn't, wear a money belt or hide the stuff really well, especially if you are venturing somewhere particularly dodgy.

• If you have an expensive watch or pair of glasses, leave them at home and buy budget replacements. It's strange how the more expensive something is the more likely it is to go missing.

• Beware of budget airlines, they will sting you for everything you do or don't do! Read the terms and conditions on the website and follow them to the letter, if anything is left a little to chance (such as bag sizes) print out the rules on the website and present them at the check in. It's getting so bad now I expect any day you'll be limited to 500 breaths of oxygen on short haul flights.

SURF CAMPS

By Rob Barber

Checking in to a decent surf camp is often the beginning of many an epic experience. Choose a good one and you can find yourself in bodyboarding heaven for the duration of your stay, with nothing much to think about than the next swell and riding waves. But it's important to do your research and choose wisely.

Very occasionally you hear a purist traveller denouncing the humble surf camp as a waste of money for the would-be bodyboard adventurer. It's taking away the travel experience of 'finding your own way', of 'making your own mistakes' and 'learning from the experiences'. While this is true to an extent, bodyboard travel has one main goal, getting waves in a far-off land … and surf camps exist to make this easier.

They offer the option to hang out with likeminded individuals, share experiences and improve your trip. They can help with everything from advice about a quiet place to sunbathe to the best bar to visit for tapas. You can involve yourself in the group atmosphere as much or as little as you want to, but there is a safe infrastructure in place with one main aim — scoring waves!

You can spend hours on Google Earth, plan your surf spot itinerary with one of the many internet surf travel sites or using guide books such as this, and you can track swells using all manner of online forecasting charts — but there is no way you can beat the knowledge of a local surf guide. As we all know, Mother Nature can be a fickle mistress, so just because Anchor Point is usually good in November, and just because a certain site says that it is going to be five foot and offshore next Thursday, you could well roll in to the car park to find it flat or a hideous 15 foot onshore mess.

That is when local guides are worth their weight in gold. They will direct you to the best spot for the conditions (and your ability level) on the day, but if the conditions change they'll know where that sand bank is that works on that tide, and the quickest and easiest way to get you there. (Often on the route that doesn't have the police check point, or via the shop that sells the tasty local delicacy for that in-between surf snack.)

Most surf camps specialise in tiered accommodation to suit your budget too, so if you are a wedged-up investment banker flying in for a deluxe long weekend of waves they'll have that penthouse suite (or the local contact to get you one). Likewise if you are a dedicated round-the-world tripper saving every rupiah, dirham and peso you can, they should have safe comfortable options to cater for you too. Check out their websites and then drop them an email with your needs.

As you're going to be surfing for most of the day you'll need fuel in your belly to make it happen. Most surf camps will have a local chef that sources the best local produce to supply you with carb-fuelled meals so you'll get the most out of the waves each day. Sure you don't have to eat at the camp, but the option of a reliable meal is there if you want it. If you are totally surfed out, the last thing you will want to be doing of an evening is gambling your health on a local 'restaurant' with a 'street chef' who by the looks of things definitely doesn't

own any pets.

Most of us can check travel review websites these days to see testimonials from other travellers. There are usually stacks on there about surf camps so investigate these recommendations and ask around. Beware of rival businesses pretending to be customers who had a 'nightmare stay' with them, and likewise, friends of the owners championing the joint as being 'heaven on earth'!

Ask around your mates at home for those who've been to the location before and can recommend certain places, or others to avoid. Decent camps get a good reputation quickly, and the bad ones soon drop off the radar. Ones that offer a good time at a fair price, keeping you safe, well fed and well surfed are out there!

OWEN PYE

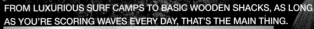

FROM LUXURIOUS SURF CAMPS TO BASIC WOODEN SHACKS, AS LONG AS YOU'RE SCORING WAVES EVERY DAY, THAT'S THE MAIN THING.

MIKE SEARLE

A SURF CAMP WILL 99 PER CENT OF THE TIME OFFER YOU THE FOLLOWING:
- Airport transfers.
- Kit repair information and contacts.
- The best priced equipment available.
- Internet availability.
- Competitively-priced food and water.
- Information on local places of interest.
- Guide to the local bars and nightlife.
- The option to hire your own vehicles or arrange local transport.
- Access to a surf photographer to shoot you ripping.
- Yoga, horse riding and a multitude of other activities if it goes flat.

The list goes on, but essentially surf camps are geared up to organise the logistics of your trip, leaving you little to do but bodyboard til you drop and enjoy the culture, climate and beach life.

BOAT TRIPS

By Rob Barber

THE INDO BOAT TRIP, SOMETHING THAT EVERY BODYBOARDER SHOULD EXPERIENCE.

If there's one type of trip worth saving the pennies for, it's an all-out boat trip to somewhere exotic. Let's face it, the idea of waking up next to a pumping empty peak and getting shacked out of your mind is the ultimate dream.

While utopian destinations like the Mentawais have become ever more crowded with numerous boat companies springing up to take advantage of the juice, there are untold numbers of unchartered archipelagos just waiting to be blown open by intrepid explorers…it all comes down to the dollar. So do your research, read the reviews, check the charts, and bite the bullet — it will be a trip worth waiting for.

HERE ARE SOME TIPS TO HELP GET YOU AMPED:

• **Pack meticulously** to make sure that you don't forget anything, from camera chargers to sun screen. If you don't take it you won't have it, simple as that. Remember above all to take spare fins, boards and leashes. The last thing you want to be doing is watching that perfect reef pass barrel down the line as you are left high and dry due to a lost flipper.

• **Be prepared physically**. Of all the types of surf trip that you can do, you are likely to be surfing more than ever before on a boat trip. If all goes well you should be mooring up next to a break each day and diving in for a wave when suits. There will be very little time out of the water, so you need your body to be ready for it.

• **Pack an open mind and a friendly attitude.** Unless you are mega rich or have managed to organise a crew of mates for your trip, you are likely to be sharing the boat with some other surfers and/or bodyboarders. That means you will be living in confined spaces with strangers and it's important that you get on from the outset, for the harmony of the boat. So just let those little niggles

wash over you … the last thing you need is a mutiny on The Bounty!

• If you are lucky enough to get a good chef you will be fed like a king and eat the most divine fish suppers that you will ever get the chance to sample. If, however, you don't like fish, or are particular about what you eat, remember to **pack some snack bars** that will supply you with plenty of energy.

• **Choose your charter carefully.** If you are going to be living at sea for a week or two you need to choose the biggest, best boat that your bucks can afford. Check the safety record and ask around to contact people that have been on the boat before. Double check the boat's schedule, and if you particularly want to hit a certain spot, make certain the boat will go there.

• **Creature comforts are essential.** Remember your iPod, some good books, a back-up pair of sunglasses, and so on. These are the things that can help you zone out during a particularly bad crossing, or if you need a bit of time away from the rest of the gang on the boat.

• **Be first on board** so that you get the pick of the beds or the cabins!

• There will likely be livestock on board that you will be eating at some point on the trip (especially in places like Indo). If you are easily attached to poultry or would rather not meet your future three-course meal, the only way to deal with it is to avoid the cooped up chickens and animals that you may see around the galley. It's just the nature of the beast.

• Go snorkeling, catch a beast of a tuna, and night dive. **Enjoy the ocean** in every way you can while you are living on it.

SWILLY

IF THE SURF GOES FLAT, THERE'S ALWAYS FISHING.

TUNGSTEN

REMEMBER YOUR LAPTOP, CHARGER, AND PLUG CONVERTER'S. BE METICULOUS WITH YOUR PACKING OR YOU'LL HAVE TO MANAGE WITH OUT.

PRO TOP TIPS:

BEN PLAYER: "The first six hours will be your worst time for seasickness on a boat. Try and stay up, sit on deck and stay focused on the horizon. Your first reaction when you feel seasick is to go below deck, but don't do it! Also, prepare for the worst and take a really good medical kit and antibiotics."

RYAN HARDY: "Be sure to bring plenty of sun cream and some good mags, DVDs, books and board games for the downtime."

MARK MCCARTHY: If you don't have sea legs then it might be worth sitting them out! A bad boat trip could put you off the ocean for a long time if you come across rough seas.

MICHAEL NOVY: Be prepared for rough weather and take something from the chemist to settle your stomach if you get seasick

ROAD TRIPS

By Owen Pye

There are few greater pleasures than you and a few mates packing up a truck and hitting the road for an epic bodyboarding trip. The image of finding some unridden gem in the middle of nowhere sure is an enticing one, but before you part with your hard-earned it's worth taking some time to get the right vehicle — it really could make the difference between life and death, especially when adventuring in remote places.

Although you won't necessarily need to stray off the blacktop to find amazing waves, you're bound to be tempted to take a quick look down a rutted coastal track to see what secrets it might yield. With this in mind, it is almost certainly worth getting a decent 4x4...not just for the extra ground clearance, but for the fact it can handle the rough stuff should the track get worse the further you go.

When checking a second-hand vehicle the first thing to do is assess

THE AFRICAN DIRT TRACK - WATCH OUT FOR DONKEYS!

MIKE SEARLE

cutting corners on.

First off, find out about the history of the vehicle. Why is it being sold? How long has the seller owned it? What did he use it for? Get as much information as you can about what has been replaced over its life before you even turn the key.

"I was on a trip in WA once and decided to head through the forest down this little dusty track after seeing a little arrowed sign on the road which just said 'beach'. After a couple of hours of dodging wild emus, the track had narrowed and deteriorated to the point where even our Toyota was struggling. We ditched it and carried onward on foot, determined to find waves. After another hour of walking through the dense bush, we finally stopped and climbed a tree to see how far we were from the waves. With a view of tens of miles — I couldn't even see the ocean yet! Sometimes you have to know when to cut your losses!"

the seller – if the person is shifty, doesn't look you in the eye, gives a limp handshake or appears vague on important questions, it's best to walk away. Similarly if something appears too good to be true, it probably is...getting a 4x4 which will see you 10,000km through some of the harshest terrain on earth is something you don't want to be

CLOSE INSPECTION

If you are satisfied everything seems legit at this stage, get out your fine tooth comb and check for the following:

• **Tyres:** Should be nail and patch-free, with deep tread and no signs of cracking or perishing rubber on the tread blocks or sidewalls. Also check the spare – if it needs one factor this into your budget,

and remember some areas of the Australian bush will require two spares to even enter in the first place.

• **Bodywork:** Make sure there is no rust on structural areas (chassis rails, subframe, sills) and whilst underneath check it is dent-free...a big impact with a rock at some point may well have damaged other parts like the engine, gearbox, exhaust, axles or driveshafts.

• **Driveshaft:** The prop-shaft which runs from the front to rear diff housing underneath should rotate free and true, check for signs of recent lubrication at either end – a failure of these U-joints (due to a lack of oil) can cause the shaft to snap, drop, and pole vault the vehicle into a lengthways flip at 60mph quicker than you would know what is happening.

• **CV Joints:** Check each of the rubber boots aren't split or leaking grease, on the test drive turn the wheel to full lock and do slow circles in both directions, there should be no clicks.

• **Exhaust:** The exhaust pipe should be hung high and tight on rubber bushes which aren't cracking. When you turn the engine on check for recently applied

putty or blowing sounds caused by small holes, if you do hear blowing, it's on borrowed time.

• **Gearbox and diff housings:** These need to be non-leaking and free of crunches, grinds and knocks. It is always worth changing the box oils before your trip anyway – who knows when it was last done. On the test drive try all gears (including reverse), making sure they are slick changes with no trouble engaging. Likewise with the high/low ratio box engage all settings in each gear and check each works with no hesitations or problems. For full four-wheel drive you may need to manually lock the hubs on the front wheels as without these engaged you'll still only be spinning the rears. Some manufacturers have auto-locking hubs, some don't, so do your research on this before testing the vehicle. Bear in mind it should always be run on two-wheel drive until you physically need four wheel drive due to lack of traction (and usually then at low speeds).

• **Suspension:** Bounce each corner firmly — the shocks should level the car on each corner after a couple. If it continues to bounce and bounce you will need to replace the shocks. Even if it levels off well enough, it is worth checking them all in case of weeping. Whilst your head is under the wheelarch make sure the springs aren't cracked or even snapped – it does happen.

• **Tow bar:** If it has one, enquire for how long – if the thing has been towing two tonne trailers all its life you could be in for a clutch or some big transmission bills, especially if it's an automatic.

• **Brakes:** Check the pads and discs have a good amount of material and life left in them and on the test drive that the callipers aren't binding. If it has anti-lock brakes check them by trying to lock up

THE SECOND THAT ALL THE MILES ON THE ROAD
SEEM WORTH IT, WHEN YOU CATCH GLIMPSE OF
A SICK NEW LINE UP.

MICKEY SMITH

OWEN PYE

OWEN PYE

LIMITED WATER
PLEASE DO NOT ASK
FOR WATER AS
REFUSAL OFTEN OFFENDS

security

ON THE ROAD BEFORE DAWN, BEFORE IT GETS TOO UNCOMFORTABLY HOT TO TRAVEL AND BEFORE ANYONE ELSE GETS IN THE WATER.

the brakes on the test drive – if it skids rather than quickly juddering to a stop, the ABS isn't working.

• **Engine:** Get as much history as you can on the engine, previous service intervals, and dates of replaced parts. All engines require regular oil and filter changes, and periodically bigger jobs such as the cam belt, radiator or water pump. Check to see if these have been done, and if so, when. Cross-reference the change dates to the mileage, and compare it to what the manufacturer-suggested mileage is for each part. If you snap an aging cam belt it will destroy your valves and potentially damage your pistons requiring an expensive rebuild, so if it is overdue get it done. If there is no record of when it was done, take off the plastic cover and check for printed writing still visible on the back of it – if it's faded and gone it's time for a change.

Check for oil or coolant leaks on the floor underneath the engine, if you

see drips try to assess from which part of the engine it's coming from. If it's dripping from the oil filter it will more than likely just be a cheap O-ring but could offer you good room for a big haggle. Likewise if an engine is sparkling clean be suspicious – it could be something is being hidden. It should be dirty and covered in a thin layer of old road grime. When you turn petrol (gasoline) engines on they should catch instantly – any longer and you may have a tiring battery, alternator, starter motor or ignition system. You could also have fueling issues. Check for the smell of petrol (gasoline)). Diesels will need the glow plugs to warm up before firing up, the requisite light on the dash should extinguish within a few seconds of turning the key a click. Once idling, listen out for whistles, knocks, taps and clunks. Check the tachometer after it has settled that it is idling at 750rpm (plus or minus 50rpm). If it's idling high

it could be a vacuum leak, carbon build up or faulty ECU or sensors. Make sure it revs cleanly with no hiccups or flat points – if it is lumpy or running rough you may have distributor, fuel and/or ignition issues. (Or worse!) On your test drive check for sounds which shouldn't be there and that it accelerates, brakes, changes gear and handles as you would expect. Make sure the temperature gauge sits halfway when warmed up and that the oil pressure isn't too high or low, it should vary from halfway to three quarters depending on load. If anything seems out of the ordinary bring it up — you may have enough room for haggling (or even enough reason to walk away).

You should also satisfy yourself that all the paperwork is in order and that the seller definitely owns the vehicle. Do some research before you leave on what's required for the country you're visiting, including things like road and emissions test certificates.

TUNE UP

Once you have bought your new ride and are looking to get it ready for the road, take it into a garage for a full service including air/fuel/oil filters, engine/gearbox/diff oil changes, fresh coolant, leads, plugs, wheel balancing, tracking and alignment. It is not only peace of mind in doing this, but it will also help improve your economy, which will suffer if you plan on installing a roof rack for:

• **Spare jerry cans of fuel –** Can extend the range between stations by hundreds of potentially life-saving miles.
• **Water containers –** For both drinking and replenishing an overheating engine after a split hose or busted radiator.
• **Spare tyres –** Expect flats.
• **Thick nylon ratchet straps –** Quickly lock everything down tight up top.
• **Lockable roof box –** Useful external storage for tent, wettie, tools, etc...
• **Roof spotlights –** Helps spot

unwelcome highway visitors and extends your nightvision by hundreds of feet.

BULL BARS / ROO BARS

Your 4x4 may already come with roo bars, but if it doesn't, see if you can get some cheap. Hitting a large animal like a cow or kangaroo is extremely dangerous for front seat occupants and can even kill — it is worth installing some big external spotlights for the front bars and roofrack so you can spot anything coming in off the hard shoulder ready for a collision. Kangaroos love to play at dawn and dusk, and roads seem a favourite hang out in certain places. If you are travelling at dusk or overnight, check in at service stations for reports from truckers of packs of roos they've spotted coming the other way.

ROAD TRIP KIT

You'll also need:
• **A decent quality tool kit –** Buy cheap,

buy twice. Always worth spending a bit more to get something that won't snap when needed the most.
• **CB Radio/giant antenna –** Can be expensive, but if you plan on going deep into the bush, it could be a life saver.
• **Fine plastic mesh –** For wrapping over the roo bars in front of your radiator, stops stone chips puncturing it and you would be surprised how quickly it can become clogged with insects, leading to overheating.
• **12v tyre compressor –** Allows you to decrease your tyre pressures if you plan on going off road or on sand, and inflate them again afterwards, all from your cigarette lighter socket. (Check the socket actually works before setting off!)
• **Mozzie netting –** You will need this spanning any windows left open overnight, you've been warned!
• **Duct tape –** Get a few rolls, the stuff can fix all but the biggest of problems.
• **Cable ties –** See above!

• **WD40 –** Can unseize bolts which have never been taken off in 20 years saving you a lot of effort, swearing, and bleeding knuckles.
• **Screen wash –** You'll need some serious stuff with you to cut through the inevitably thick glaze of splattered insects.
• **Tent –** Watch out for spiders in shoes come morning.
• **Gas stove –** Boils the water for the coffee needed for those long wheel sessions, and for hot meals of course.
• **Plates/cups/cutlery/pans/ condiments/lighter/ mobile phone car charger –** You'll always forget something.
• **Map –** Regional, with decent close up sections of any areas you plan on exploring.
• **Dash compass/thermometer –** Always handy.

PRO TOP TIPS:

RYAN HARDY: "Ensure you'll be comfortable with your clothing — hot enough/cool enough and a big refillable bottle of water."

JARED HOUSTON: "Always wear your seatbelt, and only rent cars with an iPod jack, the iTrips don't always work."

BEN PLAYER: "Never drive when you're tired! I have done it and have almost crashed a few times, but have been lucky to catch myself before veering off the road. Good people die in car accidents, so don't be one of them."

STAYING SAFE

By Owen Pye

TRAVEL INSURANCE

One thing easily forgotten (at your peril) is travel insurance. Make sure you get some sorted well before you go, and confirm (in writing if necessary) that the policy covers you for bodyboarding. Also check it covers travel delays, cancellations, curtailments, legal expenses, legal support, personal liability and the financial backup of missed and cancelled departures.

Research companies that have good reputations and if you need to make a claim keep all your receipts from every bandage and bag of drugs you needed to buy if you are struck down somewhere remote — have them signed by any officials and doctors you can, keep them safe and send them off recorded delivery within the allocated time stated in your paperwork so your insurer has no excuse to wriggle off the hook in covering you. I talk from personal experience!

TROPICAL DISEASES

Arrange to have vaccinations at least six weeks before you leave, as they may need this time to become effective. Your doctor will advise you which jabs are needed for your destination. See page 154 for useful websites.

Diseases such as malaria and dengue fever are transferable through mosquito and insect bites, and can vary from minor irritation to life-threatening illness if left untreated. Some species of mosquito have built up a natural immunity to DEET products, so the stronger repellent Incognito is recommended.

The following tips can help stop you being bitten in the first place:
• Use mosquito nets at night (as fine a

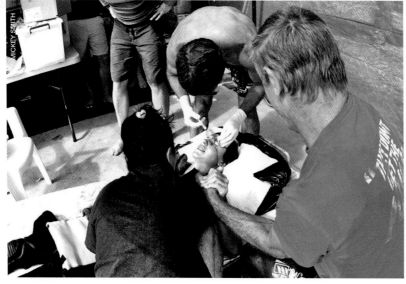

mesh as possible).
• Wear long, light-coloured clothing (mozzies are attracted to darker clothing).
• Avoid hanging around near bodies of still water (especially in the evening).
• Minimise smells, wash thoroughly and become as odour-free as possible.
• Olive oil works as a good alternative if you run out of mozzie spray.
• The chances of catching tropial diseases and ailments can be reduced by practicing good hygiene and sanitation, disinfections of food and water, and keeping your food prep areas, water supply, clothing, sheets and living areas clean.

SUNBURN

Yeah, that old chestnut. Nothing sucks more than arriving on your dream trip, paddling straight out to the waves for a long session, getting the most intense sunburn you've ever had, and sitting out

of the water in the shade with your head in a bucket of ice and aloe-vera leaves for the next week whilst you go through the hideous stages of the post-burn spiral.

Follow these tips to protect your skin and maximise your time in the waves:
• Surf early and late to avoid booging at the peak sun period of 10-3pm (when many places blow onshore anyway).
• Be aware that cloudy days don't mean you don't need suncream – the clouds do nothing but scatter the sun's UV light, and you can still burn easily.
• Regardless of your destination, bring a decent pair of sunglasses and a hat – don't be caught out. Also consider long-sleeved shirts and trousers if you are expecting to be exposed in the sun for a prolonged period.
• Beware of suncreams that claim to be waterproof and aren't – go with established surf company creams if

you are unsure. If you are fair-skinned go for the maximum protection factor and consider some sunblock/zinc cream on top to make sure you are prepared.
• Think about the areas exposed, it's not just your face, neck and arms that get blasted by the rays on a sunny day in the surf – it's always worth applying suncream to your lower back in case your rashie rises up, your legs (especially your calves) and heels, ears and hands.
• Apply suncream before and after a session to replenish the amount worn off whilst you were busting backflips in the water.
• If you do get burned, try and find an aloe vera plant, strip the leaves and squirt the gel inside onto the areas which are most affected. Wear loose-fitting clothing (or preferably none) over the redness, have cool showers and take a cool damp cloth moistened with cold water and skimmed milk to soothe the burn and build up a protein layer. Remember there is no such thing as a healthy tan, it is the just the body's response to skin damage.

SUNSTROKE

Sunstroke – or heatstroke as it is also known – is a serious condition your can face when dealing with extreme and/ or prolonged heat. It happens as your body struggles to cope with regulating its temperature to normal levels, leaving your major organs at risk, and can prove fatal. If you feel weak during or after a surf or period of intense exercise, replenish lost fluids straight away. Failure to do this can lead to heat exhaustion, which in turn can result in heatstroke.

Sunstroke is defined by a body

temperature in excess of 40°C (104°F). Reducing your core temperature is critical in this situation and can be done by removing heat-retaining clothing, immersion in cool water, strategic use of ice packs, drinking lots of water or diluted sports drinks, and finding the shade and/or good ventilation to drop your body heat back down to safe levels.

CUTS AND ABRASIONS

It is very important that you treat cuts in tropical areas as there a higher risk of infection as there are more bacteria in warm tropical seas.

• Clean the wound with fresh clean water, pick any pieces of dirt or reef from the wound with tweezers, dry it and apply antiseptic (cream, wipe or liquid).

• Dress wound with gauze or plaster skin and keep clean.

• Change the dressing at least every three days.

• Yellow pus, soreness or redness indicate that the wound is infected. Clean it out again and apply antiseptic. If the infection persists, go see a doctor or hospital.

MINOR MARINE HAZARDS

Blue Bottle/Portuguese Man-Of-War:

• DO NOT rub the affected area or apply vinegar (vinegar will cause the nematocysts to deliver more venom)

• Remove the tentacles with sea water

• Apply a dry cold compress to relieve the pain

Other jellyfish:

• As above but you may apply vinegar.

• If a Box Jellyfish or Irukanji is suspected, seek medical help immediately.

Sea urchin spines

These are very rarely poisonous but can be very painful if you step on them.

• Immerse the foot in hot water, as hot as you can bear, to relieve the pain.

• Remove as many of the spines as you can with tweezers.

• Apply antiseptic and keep wound uncovered but clean.

• The spines should dissolve after

three weeks or so but if there is pus or persistent pain visit a doctor.

HYPOTHERMIA

Hypothermia is when your body is exposed to prolonged periods of cold, and where it is unable to warm its core temperature to above 35°C (95°F). If you are planning a trip to somewhere cold, make sure you have an excellent wetsuit with a hood, gloves, socks, and somewhere set up to get warm again as quickly as possible after a surf.

The symptoms of hypothermia include not thinking or speaking properly, having trouble coordinating basic functions, amnesia, acting irrationally, shivering, and having cold, pale skin. If untreated your pulse will slow, you may suffer shallow breathing, and it can even result in your heart stopping altogether. Below a core temperature of 32°C (89.6°F) you can become unconscious, which can lead into a coma and death.

If hypothermia is suspected in someone, it is important not to expose them to too high a heat; the trick is to gently warm them, and allow their core temperature to creep back up to safe levels. Hugging them and wrapping them in sheets, towels or plastic polythene sheets if available will help, and it is important to keep the head warm.

BITES AND STINGS

While many insect bites cause nothing more than an itchy red lump, some bites and stings can trigger allergic reactions due to chemicals released in the insect's saliva or venom. If bacteria gets into the bite or sting it can cause a localised reaction, reddening further, becoming sore, filling with pus and leading to swollen glands and flu-like symptoms, so try not to scratch the bite too much and clean it with antiseptic creams or wipes. If there is a sting left in the wound, scrape it out with a card or your nail, don't try and pincer it out or you may squeeze more venom out of the sac.

Allergic reactions are caused when your body's immune system mistakes

FIN RUBS

If you feel a fin rub coming on then deal with it straight away – if left untreated it could ruin your trip.

Clean it using antiseptic, and if the skin is already broken put a plaster over it to save it getting infected. Most importantly of all, stop it been rubbed anymore. So change the type of fin you are using or use a wetsuit flipper slipper (mini neoprene sock). If the rub is around your heal/ankle area, you can buy neoprene pads that go around your ankle strap or you can sew neoprene on there. If the fin is rubbing inside the foot pocket it is possible to stick a piece of neoprene in the

ALEX WILLIAMS

FIN RUBS, THE BAIN OF EVERY BODYBOARDER'S TROPICAL TRIP.

offending area using superglue. It's been known for people to cut a hole in their fin where it rubs.

Whatever you do, don't just leave it, it will only get worse. If nothing else, put a plaster on it, then wrap duct tape round it to hold it in place.

a harmless substance as harmful, and releases natural chemicals such as histamine that can lead to swelling and itchiness.

These treatments can help reduce pain and swelling:

• Local anaesthetic spray to reduce pain

• Hydrocortisone cream applied to reduce swelling and inflammation.

• Soothing cream such as calamine lotion.

• Antihistamine cream or pills.

• Some bites or stings may require antibiotic cream or tablets depending on how bad the reaction is.

Serious allergic reactions, or anaphylaxis, will require urgent medical attention.

PRCTICAL TIPS

Before you head off make sure you meet the country's entry requirements and have the necessary visas required. Check with the Foreign Office or State Department as to potential threats in the areas in which you wish to travel — be it the onset of a natural disaster or violent political instability. It is also worth checking where the nearest embassy is located and its phone numbers and opening times.

Write your emergency contact details in your passport, commit your

passport number to memory and make a couple of photocopies of it should something happen to your original. It is important to let your family and friends know where you are going and planning on staying. Leave them your contact number, insurance policy numbers and travel itinerary. If it looks to be changing frequently it might be worth making a Google Doc and allowing your family access, so any quick changes made can be seen by them immediately.

Bring some spare US dollars for a little fund should corrupt foreign cops or checkpoint officials demand impromptu payments – US dollars are universal currency. While credit cards are a dangerous path to walk if you can't afford repayments, there is a certain peace of mind in having a spare card for you to rock up to a foreign airport after all your gear and wallet has been stolen and be able to buy a flight straight home.

It is worth carrying a spare wallet and stuffing it with business cards, old bank cards which are no longer valid and some loose change. If you do get held up, hand over the dummy wallet. Don't forget your driving licence if you want to hire a car on your trip, and familiarise yourself with local road laws and regulations which may be vastly different than what you are used to.

Stumbling upon tropical perfection

By Owen Pye

I WAS IN FIJI AND HOBBLING WITH NASTY FIN RUB. THE SESSION ON VITI LEVU THAT HAD CAUSED IT HAD BEEN WORTH IT, BUT I NEEDED A FEW DAYS OUT TO LET IT SEAL UP.

My mate Tinhead wasn't faring much better either. With trepidation he accepted he finally needed (in the end triple) root canal surgery, and one painful afternoon he succumbed to the prospect of finding some backstreet 'dentist' in Suva. After his surprisingly successful operation we bailed to a tiny island in the Lomaiviti group. You could walk around the island in ten minutes, so we set up the tent in among the coconut trees and kicked back.

One day, after the trade winds had eased into the evening, I was sure I heard the sound of waves across the lagoon. I grabbed the binoculars and scanned the horizon. Sure enough, my hopes had been confirmed — whitewater had started flicking up on the fringe reef. Excited, we quickly paid a local fisherman to take us out along the reef to look for waves.

The backdrop was stunning. Giant tropically-forested slopes rose sharply from the beach palms into the heavens behind. Traces of cloud hung in wisps around the dense canopies. Schools of angelfish and four-stripe damsels shimmered and bolted as the boat skipped across the turquoise lagoon, and we soon started getting a sense of what we had stumbled upon. Easterly swell had begun to strike, and there was a smorgasbord of lefts and rights reeling at pace. The second reef pass we approached was firing. In falling light we could see clean and warpy overhead right handers, unloading into a bowl with dubious makeability. We were amping, and convinced the bemused fisherman to get up early and take us back out there the following day.

The next day it had dropped off a bit, but was still pitching and sucking hard into a 50-metre crescent, losing size but gaining speed as it warped and wrapped around the reef faster and faster. Picking your line was crucial, speed imperative. Once you had bottom turned you had to trim at pace into the sweet spot to have any chance of making the funnelling section you had committed to. My second wave taught me this. Lazily setting up for the barrel, it sucked hard and in the blink of an eye tossed me over with the lip. I popped up missing a fin but somehow without a scratch. For hours, miles from anywhere and on the edge of the world, we swapped waves, shared stoke and struck gold.

As the tide dropped it got shallower than I had thought possible. Sitting on my board the tips of my fins were scraping the multicoloured razors, and any sneaker sets would have had us in ribbons. You didn't duckdive here so much as contort yourself into a ball and try to keep all your important bits on the inside. A while later we were waiting in a lull when we heard a strange noise build, and turned around to figure out what it was. Working their way down the jagged green valleys into the lagoon and tearing towards us in a defined wall, were raindrops the size of golf balls. Suddenly the water around us was obliterated, each impact splashed up like a pebble in a pond. Visibility dropped heavily and we could hardly even see one another. We laughed aloud and hooted, but the tropical downpour muted our sounds in the roar.

Shortly after the rain stopped the swell dropped off, and we paddled back to the boat, buzzing. The fisherman told us behind a beaming smile he had fished along that reef for 50 years and had never seen anyone ride a wave there. In homage to Tom Hanks in Castaway, we named the spot Wilson. The next day we went back but it was silent and flat, once again hiding its secret.

It's a good feeling knowing Wilson exists, warping hollow into that deep blue channel. A better feeling is knowing it will be empty when I surf it again.

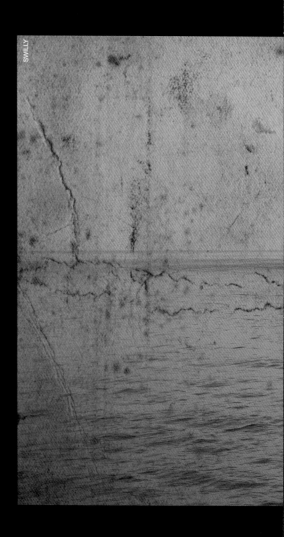

SWILLY

FITNESS

By Rob Barber

RYAN MATTICK, PREPARED FOR
ANYTHING THIS SUPERS BARREL CAN
THROW AT HIM.

A WELL-TAILORED LAND TRAINING PROGRAMME WILL HELP YOU ACHIEVE YOUR PEAK FITNESS GOALS JUST IN TIME TO BOARD THE PLANE AND HEAD OFF ON YOUR TRIP. REMEMBER, IF YOU TIME IT RIGHT YOU'LL HOPEFULLY BE SCORING ALL-TIME WAVES, SO TO BE ABLE TO TACKLE AND MAKE THE MOST OF THEM YOU'LL NEED TO BE ON TOP OF YOUR GAME!

All your hard work will have been worth it when you have every barrel to yourself once your mates have had to call it quits after six hours as they are exhausted. You will be able to paddle back out quicker than anyone else, hold your breath longer, boost higher and generally be bodyboarding better.

A properly planned programme of work each week in the run up to your trip with good progressive training principles, allowing you to bodyboard stronger, with more energy and flair when you arrive.

A training programme will help you prepare for your trip both physically and mentally, whether you want to increase your paddle power, give greater explosive speed, or just improve movement and flexibility. Charting your progress each week will help you stay focused on your goals, boosting your motivation and allowing you to see your progression.

As with any training programme, a good constructive warm-up is vital; this combined with a good cool-off section will allow you to stay injury free. The key to a proper well balanced land-based bodyboard training programme is to tailor it to suit your fitness ability. Aim for exercises and movements that will strengthen your own bodyboarding style. There's no point in just pulling your trainers on and running aimlessly for miles, you need to keep the exercises directly relevant.

In general, well-balanced training should contain some form of aerobic training like running or swimming. There should also be some form of upper body strength training using weights and resistance bands. *Important: don't just focus on your upper body and general fitness.* Your legs play a vital role in bodyboarding, they are your paddling engine, so keeping them injury free is a must. Focus on leg work that will keep your knees, ankles and hips strong.

Everybody is physically different and has varying amounts of time available to devote to training. Traditionally, the period leading up to a trip is a hectic period of cramming in work and organising things, so the earlier you start the better. You may wish to train just once a week or four times a week, it's all down to you and what you want to achieve.

A proper bodyboarding programme and diet should build strength, improve muscle power, burn fat and keep you trim by improving your aerobic performance and flexibility. Any well-balanced flexibility programme should cover all major muscle groups and be tailored to improve every part of your bodyboarding. Think about the movements that you want to achieve and replicate them in the gym or training room.

If you're training three or four times a week it will be beneficial to limit your sessions to one or two different training types and alternate them regularly. For example:

- **Monday:** Plyometrics and balance training
- **Tuesday:** Aerobic training — swim or run
- **Thursday:** Free weights and resistance bands
- **Friday:** Core strength training

A change of training type is often better than over-training. You may wish to develop additional strength using weights during the flat season and only use resistance bands for strength when the waves are good.

Changing a training programme every eight weeks or so will allow your body to stay challenged. It's good to mix things up to keep the body guessing.

Bottom line, when the waves don't cooperate or you can't get to the beach you should have a training programme in place that is specific to your body type and the goals you want to achieve for your trip. If you can, speak to your local gym instructor and aim to develop a plan between you. If you are interested in reading more on fitness, pick up a copy of The *Complete Guide to Surf Fitness* by Lee Stanbury, it's ace.

Above all, when you have the opportunity to go bodyboarding, make sure that you get out there and surf hard. It's the best training that you can get and is also the most fun.

CHRIS POWER

PRO TOP TIPS:

BEN PLAYER: "Personally I'm pretty conscious of keeping fit and eating well. Even if I don't have a goal like a trip I will try and keep fit. At the moment I'm getting right into swimming, I did training the other day and managed 3.2km in 52 minutes which is pretty good for someone that started two weeks ago!"

JARED HOUSTON: "Depends where you're going and the waves you plan on surfing, but above all else, core, core, and core! This will keep your rig looking tight, for ladies of all shapes and sizes!"

RYAN HARDY: "Be aware of the surf potential at your destination and prepare your body and skills for the condition. For example, Hawaii and Mexico demand the most fitness of anywhere, so to feel more confident in jumping straight into solid conditions, be sure to actively surf and train for at least 2-3 weeks before you arrive"

MARK MCCARTHY: Always keep a busy body and mind! I always try to ride every day, but remember it is key to train wise, not to train hard.

COLD WATER TRIPS

By Rob Barber

Well, you've manned up. You've decided to ditch the boardies for a new pair of gloves and a hood … somewhere cold and dark awaits. Despite battling hypothermia and ice on your kit each morning, one thing you invariably won't be battling on a cold water trip is a crowd.

While most boog-bound flights are being booked somewhere warm (and probably rammed) you can seek comfort in an epic trip to a bodyboarding frontier most wouldn't consider. It's really not a mad as it seems: the world's cold water locations get just as much swell as the hot ones, there are thousands of sick setups, and the scenery in places like Iceland, Canada and Alaska is stunning.

Plus, while many of your sweating brethren are copping aggro and jostling for a place in the hectic lineup of Padang

BRANDON FOSTER CARVING IN ICELAND.

Padang , praying to luck into the odd leftover shack every couple of hours, you'll be getting repeatedly slotted in some clear glass funnels for as long as you wish, followed up by a toasty warm campfire. Plus, when you get back home you'll have some real stories to tell, not just the standard 'went to Kuta, caught Chlamydia and surfed a bit.' So go on, think about heading to the far North (or the far South)

SOME TIPS FOR COLD WATER FRONTIERSMEN:

• Be sure to sort yourself out with a reputable 5/4/3mm or even 6/5/4mm wetsuit and accompanying hood, gloves and socks depending on the water temperature of your destinations. Never underestimate how crucial your kit is in cold climes.

• Bring a board suited to the water temperature with a flexible PE core, you'll need all the control you can get when the water is cold.

• Always double check the recent weather conditions in the area. It could be unseasonably cool or warm, so make sure that you pack accordingly.

• Warm food equals a warm body. When you get out of the water have a hot flask of soup or tea ready to drink. As soon as you get it inside you you'll feel the benefit immediately.

• Ensure that your neoprene wear is up to scratch — a single hole in a wetsuit sock can potentially ruin a whole trip.

• Try your fins on while wearing your wetsuit socks before you go and make sure that they're not too tight. Cramp sucks, so make sure you get a good fit before you find yourself in Alaska asking the local bear hunters if they have a spare set of fins.

• When baggage limits allow, try to travel with two wetsuits. The simple logic here is you can let one dry out as you surf in the other, meaning you will (hopefully) never have to put on an icy wet suit.

• Depending on your destination you may be able to buy the best kit locally.

So if you are going to Norway there's every chance you'll be able to buy a nice thick suit from a surf shop on the ground. Check online first and pre-order one, that way you won't have to lug too much heavy gear halfway around the world.

• Sunscreen! It can be surprising but wind burn can be almost as bad as sunburn, so protect your face or you could end up knocking around an Icelandic bar looking like a beetroot.

• Thick socks and thermal underwear is the best way to keep you warm on land. By the same token, thermal rash vests and kidney warmers can give you the boost that you need to surf for that extra 30 minutes when it's pumping.

• Of all the items of clothing that you need to take with you, make sure that you pack a beanie hat... small to squeeze in your bag and incredible for insulation on the après-surf emergency warm up.

• The length of time that you spend in freezing temperatures is limited, so make sure that you time your surf session to get the best from the conditions, you don't want to be sitting around for ages in freezing conditions waiting for the main bulk of the swell to hit.

• Warm, loose fitting clothing is the best gear to wear when you are on a cold water surf trip. It's also the easiest to get in and out of when you are half naked in a snow flurry. Think tracky bottoms, Ugg boots and hoodies, rather than skinny jeans, lace up trainers and a button up shirt. It's survival, not a fashion show.

• A changing robe is a better idea than you think, you can just jump out of your

wettie under the robe and straight in your car to drive back to your accommodation to get changed in the warm. Even better, get some waterproof seat covers for your ride and you can completely miss out the hell of getting changed in the cold altogether.

PRO TOP TIPS:

BEN PLAYER: "Make sure you are prepared to get properly cold when you go on a cold water trip. There is nothing more annoying that not having enough stuff to keep you warm, you can always take it off if you get too hot!"

JARED HOUSTON: "A new wetsuit can make a world of difference, it really is worth the spend before a trip to a cold water destination. Plus, remember to take a thinner, more flexible board too."

RYAN HARDY: "Make sure you get kitted with wetties thick enough that you won't be shivering after half an hour and boards that are a bit more flexible and/ or worn in, to compensate for the cold water 'rockboard' syndrome."

MARK MCCARTHY: A good wetsuit comes in useful makes a HUGE difference. I would rather go for a thinner suit with a more flexible fit, but once you start feeling the cold it gets hard to ride at your best.

MICHAEL NOVY: Pack plenty of clothes and plenty of rubber! even if you have to wear a hood or booties to keep warm. Its never fun getting so cold that you can surf because your hands are to numb!

IF YOU EVER HEAD TO ICELAND, MAKE SURE YOU'VE
GOT A GOOD WETSUIT WITH NO HOLES IN IT OR
YOU'LL BE IN A WHOLE WORLD OF PAIN.

DEST-
INATIONS

HOW TO USE THIS GUIDE

The purpose of this book is to fuel your imagination.
It is not intended as a comprehensive guide to every
bodyboarding spot in the world. Rather it is a starting
point for you, a "bucket list" of places any booger would
aspire to surf at some point in their life. For this reason
we haven't supplied any detailed location maps on each
of the spots as some of them are secret or semi-secret.
We figure that, with the huge amount of information
available on the internet, you will be able to do some
detailed research if you so wish. We hope we will give
you with the inspiration to get out there and explore and
score!

CALIFORNIA//116

EAST COAST
USA//121

MEXICO//142

CARIBB
//138

HAWAII//122

CENTRAL AMERICA //136

PACIFIC ISLANDS//102

BRAZIL

CHILE//130

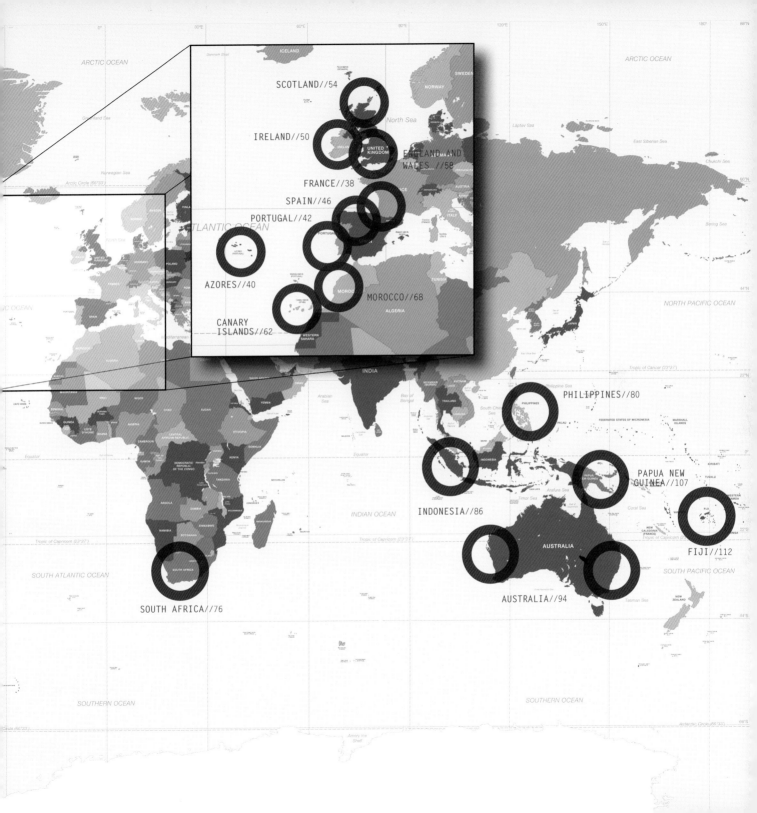

SCOTLAND//54

IRELAND//50

UNITED KINGDOM

ENGLAND AND WALES //58

FRANCE//38

SPAIN//46

PORTUGAL//42

AZORES//40

MOROCCO//68

CANARY ISLANDS//62

PHILIPPINES//80

INDONESIA//86

PAPUA NEW GUINEA//107

FIJI//112

SOUTH AFRICA//76

AUSTRALIA//94

FRANCE

AWESOME BEACHBREAKS AND BEAUTIFUL WOMEN.

LANGUAGE.....**FRENCH**
MAIN AIRPORT.....**CHARLES DE GAULLE INTERNATIONAL AIRPORT (CDG)**
CURRENCY.....**EURO**
SWELL SEASON.....**YEAR ROUND**
WATER TEMP.....**6C-28C**

OUTLINE

France is one of the largest countries in Europe with a long coastline which stretches from the top of the English Channel right down to the border of Spain at the bottom of the Bay of Biscay. While the rocky north west is much more reminiscent of Cornwall or Northern Spain with its coves and reefs, the famous southern stretch of the Bay of Biscay consists of more than 120 miles of straight west-facing beach, endless sand

dunes, backed by peaceful pine forests (ordered by Napoleon to be planted to tame this boggy low-lying land).

France has been integral to the development of surfing in Europe, and has long been a staple summer bodyboard destination with perfect weather, golden sands, warm water and open-ocean swell, unhindered by a continental shelf.

BREAKS

Just off the coast of Hossegor there is a deep ocean trench which serves to funnel swell into the area and gives the breaks of Biscay more power and punch, making the beachie waves of southern France some of the best in the world, offering up world class peak after world class peak. Due to the shifting nature of sandbanks though, sick spots can pop up from nowhere to break perfectly for a few weeks at a certain state of the tide before quietening down again, so it takes a little

IF YOU SCORE GOOD WEATHER, GOOD WAVES AND A GOOD BANK. THERE IS NO BETTER PLACE TO BE THAN SOUTH WEST FRANCE.

bit of local knowledge to know where is working best. The ability to get out from the Hossegor mêlée will be sure to yield uncrowded barrels, as green swell lines pumped from North Atlantic lows barrel under clear blue skies for as far as the eye can see. Heading north up the coast beyond Bordeaux there are good waves too, but without the same power. Further north still, Brittany has waves aplenty with coves and reefs all round its coastline offering variety and thinner crowds.

BOOGVIBE

The bodyboarding scene in France is big and ever-growing with generous government funding and a healthy contest scene. The younger generation rips, and have genuine reason to think they can make it too, with international superstars like backflip-machine Pierre Louis Costes and 2010 World Champion

ROCK FOOD AN INSTITUTION IN THE FRENCH SURFING COMMUNITY.

"The Hossegor area is really good because it picks up almost any swell. You can surf every day, chasing the best sand banks depending on swell size and wind direction. Summer is a bit crowded but there are kilometres of empty beaches to the north. Winter is not too harsh. The after surf is always good with very some excellent restaurants and nice places to have a drink." - Mathieu Desaphie

CAPBRETON

South of Capbreton is a stretch of beachbreak peaks which churn out barrel after barrel in front of giant upturned German wartime bunkers. One of the best peaks is located near VVF (VVF is a chain of French holiday villages which dot the coast). There will be crowds, especially in the summer, but for green tubular shacks and fun peaks ready to offer you a cover up and a ramp it is definitely worth a paddle out

VVF SERVING UP SOME LATE SUMMER PERFECTION.

LA GRAVIERE

If the banks are lined up nicely, La Graviere is one of the all-time great beachies. La Grav is hollow and heavy, breaking left and right throughout all tides over a sandbar which trips up the deepwater swell with reef-like power. La Grav works throughout all tides and can get very heavy in the shorey on high. Expect a busy lineup (and riddled with stand-ups during contest season) but all the hassle is forgiven with La Grav when you pull into one of its famous barrels, which'll reel and peel just like Puerto. Located just north of Hossegor centre, it works best on a west swell with an east wind.

PABLO PRIETO PULLS IN TO A
MONSTER HOSSEGOR CAVERN.

Amaury Lavernhe proudly flying the French flag at IBA tour stops around the world.

With photos of boogers scooping into gaping green caves plastered across the pages of international sponge mags for decades, it is no wonder the warm water lineups of the 'south west corner' have become packed — but with such a stretch of open coast, finding a hollow empty peak is still a lot easier here than anywhere else.

FRANCE TRAVEL TIPS

Barrels, beachies, babes, boogying, beers, berets, baguettes and a beating sun all blend beautifully in the annual Hossegor circus, which gets better the later you leave it. By autumn many of the crowds have started to pack up as increasing swell lines start to make an appearance. If the local throngs are still too much for you though, perfectly uncrowded tubular pits await you further up the infinite coast if you have a tent and an urge to explore.

Before your trip it is worth learning a little bit of French, if only to show you have made an effort.

Avoid leaving valuables on display in cars or in tents. Break-ins do happen, and nothing sucks more than coming back from scoring a session of 50 heaving bazzas to find you have no clothes, wallet or passport. Camping is still the go though — it's fairly cheap and there are dozens of good campsites in the shade of the forests behind the beaches. Although camping rough is frowned upon, the cops tend to turn

MIKE SEARLE

IF ONE SPOT STOPS FIRING OR GETS TOO CROWDED, THERE'S USUALLY ANOTHER SANDBAR DOWN THE BEACH.

"La Graviere is amazing. It's made for Bodyboarding with big barrels and good beatings dished out in equal measure. It is in Hossegor just right of Rockfood and when the swell is right you can have some really hollow waves right at the shore. It is one of those waves that can handle big swells. If it is too big everywhere else and there are no sandbanks to hold it, head to La Grav' it's the place to score huge pits!" - Pablo Prieto

a blind eye to it provided you keep a low profile, and there are numerous hidden areas in the forest where you can park up and camp out. Indeed many of the beach car parks are full of surfers' camper vans at night, and it's a great way to make the early! If you like a bit more comfort there are many apartments to rent, but in the holiday season of July and August they will be booked up and expensive.

Unfortunately the directional nature of the west-facing coastline in the south means when it's onshore, it's onshore everywhere. Luckily there are a host of other things to keep you busy; be it sampling the European coffee-and-croissant café culture, indulging in fanciful foods or joining the long queue of sunburned foreign blokes shouting poor French chat up lines to the barely-clad goddesses in the Hossegor nightclubs.

There are loads of surf shops in town so don't worry too much if something snaps or you forget a piece of kit, you'll find a replacement quickly. If you have a little time before or after your boog trip, the snowboarding in the nearby Pyrenees Mountains is excellent, and is best from December to March.

Part of the EU, French currency is in euros and international flights pour into Paris, with the regional airport at Biarritz the quickest way of getting to the waves. The transport network is good throughout the country though if you plan to stay on land and see the beautiful countryside en route.

MIKE SEARLE

IT'S NOT ALL BARRELS. THERE ARE PLENTY OF RAMPS TO PLUNDERED TOO.

PORTUGAL

BODYBOARDING RULES IN THIS NORTH ATLANTIC SWELL MAGNET

LANGUAGE.....**PORTUGUESE**
MAIN AIRPORT.....**LISBON PORTELA AIRPORT (LIS)**
CURRENCY.....**EURO**
SWELL SEASON.....**YEAR ROUND, BEST SEPT-APR**
WATER TEMP.....**14C-25C**

OUTLINE

Portugal is situated west of Spain on the western fringe of the Iberian Peninsula. Rich in culture and history, this small seafaring nation has the ocean in its DNA, with its explorers roving far and wide in medieval times when most people thought the globe was flat. Bodyboarding has really taken off in Portugal, and is at least as popular as surfing.

The riches Portugal plundered from the New World are now largely forgotten, and it was only in 1974 that a military dictatorship was overthrown. Membership of the European Union has brought prosperity, but Portugal's dark past is still visible in the cracks and dirty edges of its new suburbs and infrastructure, and is unfortunately also seen in the poor water quality near the city beaches, especially Porto in the north. Away from these, the coastline is diverse, the surf aplenty and the climate perfect for bodyboarding and exploring new spots. Further afield, the mid-Atlantic Azores are a stunningly beautiful wave-drenched haven a two-hour flight from the capitol Lisbon.

BREAKS

The Portuguese coastline is littered with variety, and prone to powerful swells from the south right round to the north. From points, reefs and beachies, to wedges, rivermouths and shories, you can find almost every type of wave in Portugal, especially in the southern half of the country, which sees an influx of barrel-hunting travellers when the autumn swells start to light up the coastline. In the far south, the Algarve's south-facing coastline turns on when big swells and northerly winds abound in the winter months. If the chart looks promising, a quick trip to the exposed Azores can also satisfy the reef-hunters who want some raw Atlantic swells and some frontier slabs.

BOOGVIBE

Portugal is buzzing with a hotbed of bodyboarding talent, with many locals absolute rippers. This charge-hard attitude has given them a great deal of respect from the surfers, who seem quite happy to share the lineups and swap waves with bodyboarders. With so many awesome shorey barrels and sections to learn their trade on, it is no wonder the IBA world tour has seen an influx of Portuguese riders stake their claim in recent years. Bodyboarding in Portugal is a booming industry, with a solid national magazine—*Vert*. The feather in its cap is the Sintra Portugal Pro; an IBA world tour stop held each year with the world's best riders putting on a show to huge crowds lining the beach.

PORTUGAL TRAVEL TIPS

Although many of the better known spots can get congested, many local boogers won't paddle out til late morning, so wake up early to get the uncrowded glass to yourself. Strangely, when it rains the lineup thins out quickly too, so if it does look like a rain shower is coming in, get ready to have the peak become a lot more profitable… at least until it brightens up. Off the beaten track are many empty spots, so get out there to sample the lesser-known delicacies.

Portugal is a generally a friendly location without a great deal of hassle, but the usual rules apply with not dropping in or paddling out with an attitude — some violence has been known to erupt. Be respectful, as you would want to be treated on your home turf.

Autumn is by far the best time to surf in Portugal, although just because the weather is still warm don't expect the sea to join in – you'll need to bring a 3/2. Portugal's currency is in Euros, and super-cheap flights can be had by budget European airlines to Porto and Lisbon from most major airline hubs. A quick, smooth and hassle-free train connects the two cities, and within a few hours you'll be getting your froth on.

ACCORDING TO PIERRE LOUIS COSTES
"NAZARE IS A VERY CHALLENGING PLACE, ALONG WITH PUERTO ESCONDIDO IT IS THE BIGGEST BEACH BREAK I HAVE EVER SURFED"

NAZARE

Rapidly gaining notoriety as one of the best and most powerful beachbreaks in Portugal, in part due to a unique offshore deepwater trench which funnels incoming swell into the beach with greater power than surrounding areas. A heavy, brutal beachie, Nazare lays down hollow rights and lefts which break with weight. Although it is open to swells from the north right round to the south west, it is the west swells which take full advantage of the underwater topography. It's offshore on an east wind and works throughout the tides.

WILL BAILEY

HOME TO SOME OF THE MOST FIERCELY COMPETITIVE BODYBOARDERS ON EARTH, SUPERTUBOS OFFERS SOME INCREDIBLE BARRELS AND RAMPS.

SUPERTUBES

The Portuguese Pipeline breaks over a punishingly shallow sandbank and can handle triple overhead plus. It works best around mid tide and delivers fast, hollow barrels to scoop into and boost out of. Beware though, there is a fine line here between a deep makeable keg and a bone-crunching closeout, especially when it's big. Depending on the swell direction Supertubes unloads both left and right, and works on S/SW/W/NW swell and is best on a NE wind. Seeing as it is a world-class beachie there will almost always be crowds when it's on and the local bodyboarders are well known to be some of the most competitive and aggressive in the world.

LUCIA GRIGGI

LUCIA GRIGGI

MICKEY SMITH

BRENDAN NEWTON SCORED IN THE AZORES.

SANTA CATARINA, AZORES

A slabby A-frame reef on the east coast of Terceira, Santa Catarina breaks both ways with a better right that can give fast heavy tubes over a sharp rock bottom. It works best on a mid tide and can handle decent sized swell (when not variable multi-directional windchop of intermittent size and period). The rocky and wild Azores sit right in the middle of the North Atlantic, and as such is a sitting duck for passing northern lows which can either pelt the islands with uninviting windswell or wrap lines down the east coast lighting up several spots, of which Santa Catarina is most renowned. There is a small take-off zone at the reef and the locals are pretty protective (having been known to forcibly ban cameras from the spot when it's on). Luck into the peak by yourself though and you should have some powerful Atlantic bombs to play with.

"The world has changed a lot in the last couple of years, but Portugal still has the ability to offer the simplicity of the good life. Hang around on a surf trip and you will be amazed by the quality and diversity of the sport. Reefs, point-breaks and even beach-breaks that can produce waves like Pipeline. Ericeira and Peniche are by far the best options, but the warm waters and weather situated in the south are also a good option. From north to south, you will find easy-going people that are always glad to help you, no matter what language you speak. Save a few bucks and enjoy a different culture with awesome visuals everywhere." - Toze Fonseca, editor of Vert Magazine.

"Portugal is a destination with an endless variety of waves. Portugal's ancient path through history has forged one of the most colourful, culturally rich yet modern cities in Europe. The Lisbon area has a great nightlife, good waves and romantic scenery attracting people from all walks of life from across Europe, making it a hub for travellers, tourists, and locals who are looking for a time well spent." — Sacha Specker.

"Santa Catarina is basically a heavy A-frame slab, perfect for bodyboarding, but the locals can be a bit funny about filming so be wary of that...there are loads of other waves around too, but they are all quite raw with heavy paddle outs." Damian prisk

MICKEY SMITH

BRENDAN NEWTON TWEAKS AN INVERT AT SAN MIGUEL, ANOTHER SLAB IN THE AZORES.

MICKEY SMITH

SANTA CATARINA SALUTATION.

THE COAST AROUND
PORTUGAL'S CAPITAL CITY
LISBON HAS A HUGE VARIETY
OF BREAKS. COSTA DA
CAPARICA SHOREY.

SPAIN

AMAZING FOOD, STUNNING LANDSCAPES, SUBLIME WAVES AND CULTURE

LANGUAGE.....**SPANISH**
MAIN AIRPORT.....**SONDICA AIRPORT (BIO)**
CURRENCY.....**EURO**
SWELL SEASON.....**YEAR ROUND, BEST SEPT-OCT**
WATER TEMP.....**12C-23C**

OUTLINE

Spain occupies the majority of the Iberian Peninsula, but due to the existence of Portugal doesn't have much west-facing Atlantic coastline. It does, however, have a healthy stretch of north-facing coast which picks up swells coming down from distant northern lows. Stretching from the French border at the south east corner of the Bay of Biscay right round to the west-facing border of Portugal, the entire length is battered by all the North Atlantic can throw at it, and has a multitude of spots perfect for bodyboarding with rivermouths, slabs and wedges.

Spain also has a smaller 150-mile stretch of SW-facing coastline in Andalucía, sandwiched warmly between Portugal and the most north-westerly tip of Africa. This stretch has a totally different feel from the greener, wetter, Celtic landscape of the north coast, featuring dry and dusty beaches and points, similar to Morocco, just eight miles distant across the mouth of the Mediterranean.

ROB HAZELWOOD

PICK A HIGH LINE AND RACE AT FULL SPEED AHEAD, THAT'S WHAT MUNDAKA IS ALL ABOUT.

BREAKS

The north coast is a playground of different bodyboarding spots, from grinding points and reeling rivermouths to heavy slabs and peaky coves and wedges. The variety of the coastline and consistency of N/NW swell sees regular waves going off at a smorgasbord of spots along the stretch, with cool clear water and beautiful surroundings.

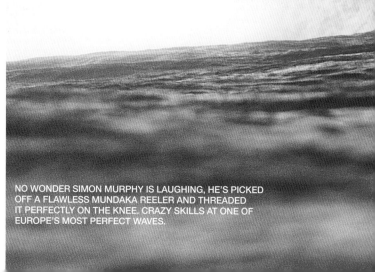

NO WONDER SIMON MURPHY IS LAUGHING, HE'S PICKED OFF A FLAWLESS MUNDAKA REELER AND THREADED IT PERFECTLY ON THE KNEE. CRAZY SKILLS AT ONE OF EUROPE'S MOST PERFECT WAVES.

MUNDAKA

The best rivermouth wave in Europe, if not the world. The famous left hander breaks like a reef over a sandbank on the western side of the Ria de Mundaka. This shallow wonder powerfully reels for hundreds of metres and can handle swell of triple/quadruple overhead with mechanical consistency. Expect big crowds, fast barrels and a fair bit of attitude by the locals, who rip and have to put up with every man, his dog and its fleas when the charts line up. Works best on a sizey N/NW swell with south winds. Jump in from the harbour and get out on the rocks on the south side of the harbour after your bazfest.

"We have waves every day in Spain, not always big, barrelling perfect waves, but always enough to go bodyboarding and have an enjoyable session. The bodyboarders are friendly but competitive which can be really good for your riding." - Alex Uranga

PLAYA DE ANDRIN

One of the best kept boog secrets on the whole coast, Playa de Andrin is nestled on the eastern edge of the stunning Asturias coast. The little horseshoe bay is home to some amazing A-frame wedges, caused by dual-angle refracted swells which wrap in around Isla de Ballota, a rocky outcrop a few hundred metres off the beach. A little bodyboarding nugget, the wedgey peak at Andrin has sick tube and punchy ramp combos which needs a medium swell to make the magic happen. The local boogers are friendly if treated well, and the vibe is good. S/SE winds are offshore in this quiet little bay, which works on all tides in both directions.

JAKUE ANDITOKOETXEA

CROSS THE BORDER FROM FRANCE AND HEAD SOUTH, SCOUR THE COASTLINE, THERE ARE STACKS OF SPOTS TO FIND, OFTEN CROWD FREE LIKE THIS GEM.

BOOGVIBE

The boogvibe in Spain is growing, with some Spanish bodyboarders appearing on the IBA world tour. With such a variety of spots on the mainland though it is no wonder that riders such as top Bilbao-born WWT rider Eunate Aguirre have progressed onto the global scene in the way they have. Although the general vibe is laid back in Northern Spain, good manners are expected in the water – don't drop in, respect the locals, paddle out with a big grin and you'll be welcomed soon enough.

SPAIN TRAVEL TIPS

Travelling in northern Spain is generally a delight, with beautiful scenery, consistent surf and endless breaks. However, tensions have risen at certain well-known spots, and car crime is sadly not uncommon. Make sure you leave nothing on display and try not to make it obvious you are travelling for waves with bumper stickers, surf mags on the dash and blocks of wax melting into the carpets – it is asking for a break in.

The food in Northern Spain is absolutely exquisite, with fresh seafood, family recipes and a plethora of tapas (delicious bar snacks) widely available. The culture here is vibrant, and while there are colourful parties which stretch long into the night, there are also respected local traditions which haven't

changed for hundreds of years. Learn some Spanish to make life easier before you go – it shows you have made an effort, which not only helps when you want to buy some bread, but could also be of use in the water should you need to diffuse a situation.

Spain is part of the EU and the currency is in Euros. There are many cheap European flights into Madrid, although Bilbao is the easiest port of call to the north coast. Connecting flights from other European destinations such as the UK will give you

"Mundaka offers you the possibility of getting one of the longest barrels of your life, but everyone knows when it's on, so don't expect to surf it by yourself. To get a good wave you have to be able to spin around at the last second and drop into a late section. There is always someone sitting deeper than you but they may fall off on the hectic takeoff or not make a barrel, then it is your turn to enjoy the experience." - Pablo Prieto

a broader range of more regional airports. If you come in by car from France the main route is the E5/E70 motorway towards San Sebastian. Further west the N-632 sticks you close to the coast. Ferries from the UK ports of Portsmouth and Plymouth also run services to Bilbao and Santander respectively, which will usually cost several hundred euros but deposit you right into the heart of the action.

MUNDAKA'S REELING PERFECTION.

IRELAND

HEAVING SLABS, BLACK BEER AND GREEN HILLS

LANGUAGE.....**ENGLISH**
MAIN AIRPORT.....**DUBLIN INTERNATIONAL AIRPORT (DUB)**
CURRENCY.....**EURO**
SWELL SEASON.....**YEAR ROUND, BEST SEP-MAY**
WATER TEMP.....**7C-17C**

OUTLINE

The island of Ireland sits on the northwest edge of Europe and soaks up all the raw North Atlantic swell which roars east from tracking low pressures off the US east coast and down from the Arctic north. The breaks which stretch down the west coast of Ireland are perfectly set up for bodyboarding, with sick slabs and reefs waiting to churn out their guts for willing barrel-hunters.

The setups of Ireland have long been known to the locals, but it has only been over the last ten years that the wider bodyboarding world has had the privilege of seeing what happens on the Emerald Isle's west coast when long-period groundswell strikes the shallow strata in the land that time forgot. The water is cold, the air is cold, but the welcome will be warm and the waves as heavy as anywhere.

BREAKS

Ireland has numerous top breaks, from the hidden giant slabs of the cliffs near Lahinch to better-known reefs of the north at Bundoran and Easkey. There are a few fun beachies, notably the wedgy Tullan Strand near Bundoran, and every nook and cranny of the coastline will yield new spots, some of which can even be offshore on the prevailing southwesterlies due to the intricate shape of the coast. This variance means there will almost always be somewhere working, known or not. Crowding at top spots has become an issue in recent years due to the growth of Irish surfing, but arrive with a mellow vibe and tempers shouldn't rise. Pack a tent and a thick wetsuit, and let the lanes of Ireland's west coast lead you on a very rewarding surf trip.

"Ireland is God's country. Long flowing green hills, constantly flowing Guinness, and big flowing barrels! Ireland's surf breaks are really perfect for bodyboarding. With most of the waves being powerful deep-water slabs that either heave and barrel hard, or wrap around into a big bowl, it is pretty heavenly to get in the water even when it is ice cold. It will take some searching if you're not from the area, but all the locals are absolute legends and are happy to show you a good time if there's only one or two of you." — Jase Finlay

BUMBALOIDS

A fast, shallow, hollow, heavy lefthand slab just south of Lahinch which locks you in and spits you out in a fit of fury. Bumbaloids can be quite fickle but is a booger's dream slab when it's on, giving throaty kegs and some hideous beatdowns should you get it wrong. It needs a high tide with west swell and east winds to do its thing. A mutant, 'loids can get extremely gnarly and demand the very best from your ability.

ONE OF THE FIRST OF MANY AUSSIES TO SCORE IRELAND'S GEMS, MATT LACKEY RIDES BACKSIDE THROUGH ONE OF THE HEAVIEST SLABS FOUND TO DATE, BUMBALOIDS.

MICKEY SMITH

RILEY'S

One of the heaviest slabs found in Europe, Riley's is a serious left hander which breaks with all the power of the Canaries and then some. It is thick, pitches fast and churns inside out at the base of an unforgiving rock slab which angles back into the action. It holds big swell and unloads onto the shallow shelf with a fearsome barrel which requires complete commitment and a perfect line. Riley's either gives you a heaving barrel which will stick in your mind forever, or a punishing and dangerous wipeout into an impact zone you want absolutely no interest in being anywhere near. 'Somewhere' near Lahinch, it works best around high tide with east winds.

BOOGVIBE

With the lid blown off Ireland's world class waves in the last few years, the bodyboarding population in Eire (the southern Irish nation which is independent of the UK) has increased dramatically with many a booger taking the trip over the Irish Sea to see what all the fuss is about. Many of the riders you meet will have been many times before, with some upping sticks to permanently move out there, such are the consistency and quality of the waves on offer. In winter it gets bleak, with only a hardened few remaining to tough it out with 6mm wetties, hoods and jet skis, but in the marginally warmer seasons expect glassy swells of more manageable size backed by a beautiful countryside and warm hospitality to take the edge off the North Atlantic chill.

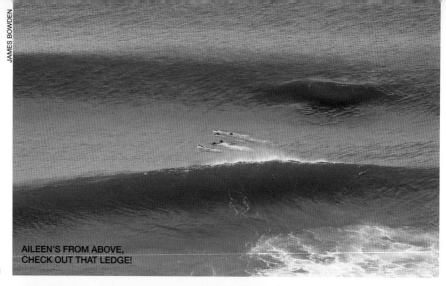

JAMES BOWDEN

AILEEN'S FROM ABOVE, CHECK OUT THAT LEDGE!

BUNDORAN PEAK

A classic A-frame reef in front of the seaside town of Bundoran, with a short right and predominant left which works best at low tide and can hold sizey swell, though expect crowds when it starts to work. When it's on you can look forward to a decent barrel and whackable wall going either way over a shallow flat reef bottom, with the left being the longer option. The spot has been in danger of a marina development for several years, but it has not yet been finalised. The Peak works best at headhigh plus, on a W/NW swell and SE wind.

ESTPIX

CROWDED WHEN IT'S ON, BUT SUCH A FUN WAVE. BUNDORAN PEAK.

MICKEY SMITH

JASON FEAST

ONE OF MANY SICK WAVES IN THE EASKEY AREA, THE RIGHT SERVES UP SOME FAST WALLY RIDES AND THE ODD AIR BOWL.

EASKEY RIGHT

A renowned reef west of Sligo which works best in northwesterly swells of all sizes. Opposite from the smaller Easkey Left, the pair are a go-to destination for locals and travellers alike due to their consistency and quality. Offshore on a south wind, Easkey Right is quite an easy reef which isn't particularly heavy but offers long barrels when the factors all line up. Works best at low tide and can give 100metre rides, although expect company in the water.

IRELAND TRAVEL TIPS

Pack a tent if you are on a budget, and a raincoat. The weather is notorious for changing quickly, don't plan a trip here and expect to stay dry on land. Be humble at the busier spots and make friends with the locals in the pub of an evening, if you're lucky you may get the nod from a farmer who'll let you pitch your tent up in a killer spot for a pint of the black stuff.

The lanes of the west coast of Ireland are narrow and twisty, so be considerate with where you leave your car; farmers who can't get past have been known to tow those cars blocking roads, so be considerate. Likewise, show goodwill when getting to the sea, many of the spots are accessible across private land, so shut gates and don't damage fences or walls, this will help keep landowners content to continue to allow bodyboarders access to their fix.

Ireland is part of the EU and as such its currency is in euros. Prices of B&Bs will hike in the summer, so consider making the trip in the autumn, when the land crowds disperse as the swells roll. There are many budget airlines which offer cheap services to and from the UK, or alternatively catch a ferry from Pembrokeshire, Holyhead or even France for varying prices. If you do take a car, expect potholes, cows and delays, so chill and enjoy the views – they are magnificent.

AILEEN'S

One of Ireland's top big wave spots, Aileen's offers up huge round right
hand barrels which boom with a bone-crunching detonation at the base of
the 800ft Cliffs of Moher, north of Lahinch. Somewhat reminiscent of
Maverick's, Aileen's needs a big swell to work properly, but will give
you top-to-bottom tubes you could fit a bus in. Recommended equipment
for tackling Aileen's on such a day is a jetski, buoyancy aid, medically-
trained tow crew, on-call helicopter and a mate at the coastguard.

GEORGE FRANKLIN TAKES THE DROP
AS AILEEN'S HITS THE LEDGE.

"Ireland was a real eye opener, the old school castles and green fields running down onto reef
platforms were just amazing. The tip for Ireland is to really study the weather maps and be onto
the tides, some waves can come to life for only two hours in the day, but once everything comes
together you will be getting some serious reef barrels." — Matt Lackey

SCOTLAND

A MYSTIC LAND OF EMPTY COLD WATER CAVES AND EPIC ARCTIC SWELLS

LANGUAGE.....**ENGLISH / SCOTTISH GAELIC**
MAIN AIRPORT.....**GLASGOW INTERNATIONAL AIRPORT (GLA)**
CURRENCY.....**BRITISH POUND STERLING**
SWELL SEASON.....**YEAR ROUND, BEST SEP-MAY**
WATER TEMP.....**4C-15C**

OUTLINE

Scotland is a wild and beautiful country atop the northern tip of the UK, with stunning ancient landscapes, a long and varied coastline and hundreds of unexplored offshore islands. It is a land of tradition, heritage and history, and is battered by large cold swells when low pressures take hold out in the Arctic Sea.

In contrast to most of the mountainous north of Scotland, the region of Caithness is flat with very few trees, and is known as one of Europe's last wildernesses. It has an underlying geology of flagstone and thanks to these flat rocks this area is home to slab reef after slab reef, mostly in the vicinity of the town of Thurso. There are also countless good setups all around the mainland and across the disparate offshore islands if you are up for some lonely exploration.

Local surfers are some of the most hardcore riders in the world...when it's a howling winter's day with only a few hours of daylight and a solid north swell arrives, you need a certain disposition to crack the ice off your wettie and brave sizey Arctic chunks over shallow slabs in the semi-darkness with no-one else out. In the summer months, if you luck into some swell, you can surf well past midnight as northern Scotland has four hours more daylight than London.

BREAKS

Scottish breaks are predominantly reefs and points, but there are also plenty of decent beachies and rivermouths too, able to break off many swell directions from south west right round to south east. The most renowned spot is Thurso East in the centre of the region's capital of Thurso, a shallow flagstone righthander which holds large swell and is a magnet for travelling spongers who have half an eye on the charts of any Arctic low. A few weeks spent exploring any stretch of Scottish coast will be almost certain to yield new spots, no doubt slabbing onto a shallow shelf without a soul in sight.

BOOGVIBE

Scotland doesn't have a huge bodyboarding culture,

BAGPIPES IS DEFINITELY A CONTENDER FOR THE BEST LEFTHANDER IN THE BRITISH ISLES. JASE FINLAY LAUNCHES OUT OF THE BOWL.

SHARPY

BAGPIPES

A super-heavy left hand reef which detonates onto a stone shelf before unwinding itself into a virtually dry bowl. A few miles from Thurso, Baggies works best at low tide but has been known to break on spring highs too. On the right swell direction the end bowl comes at you almost square-on, enabling big boosts to be smacked straight off the section. Can hold a massive swell and works best on a S/SE wind to groom the beast as it sheds its load with a power similar to any of the Canarian breaks on its day.

MICKEY SMITH

THURSO EAST LIVES UP TO ITS
REPUTATION AS THE COLD WATER NIAS.

THURSO EAST

The grand old girl has long been the main destination for Scottish trips, and for good reason. The 'cold water Nias' holds massive W/NW/N swell and peels long, deep, right hand tubes, propped up in icy offshores. Although a swell with more east will see long point-like walls, the more westerly the swell the hollower it gets, so keep an eye on those NW lines wrapping around from the North Atlantic. Barrels here are dark beasts — the sea is stained the colour of dark tea by the peat washed out in the Thurso River — and wipeouts heavy. The take off is pretty easy, but things get more critical once you've bottom turned and it breaks over the shallow kelp-covered rock ledges. It can be one of the longest, fastest barrels in Europe when it's on, with a SE wind being offshore. Paddle out with the aid of the Thurso River, which will deliver you to the lineup with dry hair, even on the big days.

THE BROWN WATER IS DUE TO THE PEAT
WASHING OUT OF THE RIVER.

ANOTHER EMPTY SCOTTISH PEAK UNLOADS OVER FLAGSTONE REEF.

SHARP

> "Scotland has a ton of reef and point breaks that are all hollow and fun. There are a lot of decent waves within close proximity that basically go unridden a lot of the year. It's pretty damn cold up Scotland way, but is well worth the adventure is you are keen for consistent swells and a range of wave choices which are all pretty much next to each other." — Jase Finlay

BRIMMS NESS BOWL

The Bowl is the heaviest of a trio of spots at Brimms Ness (the others being Brimms Ness Point, and the Cove) which scoops up any swell going and drops it into a heaving right hand slab which jacks up quickly over a barnacle-covered slate ledge and delivers fast, slabbing barrels, perfect for bodyboarding. A southerly wind is offshore, although the spot is exposed and is more susceptible to changing winds. Find it by driving west out of Thurso and following the signs off the main road. Park at the farm but be considerate, you are on private land.

SEAMUS MAKIM

WHEN BRIMMS BOWL IS FIRING IT CAN OFFER SOME OF THE CRAZIEST BARRELS IN THE AREA. BRAD JACKSON IN THE THICK OF IT.

but its waves are screaming out for one. That's not to say it's vacant, there are some hardened boogers up here which get on it with a hardy resolve when there is swell, but most people you will spot in the water will be hood-and-bootied surfers. Obviously the cold water and sheer remoteness make it a tough trip, but suck it up and ye shall find — there are some spots up here which are just custom-built for bodyboarding.

SCOTLAND TRAVEL TIPS

Scotland is without doubt a wild destination; bring warm clothes, a big flask of hot stuff and a hunger to find some hidden gems, booming away on the northern periphery of the world. In the colder seasons bring a thick wetsuit, hood and gloves, or you may find your sessions being cut short before your body temperature plummets. A PE board

is also recommended. There's an old saying that you can experience all four seasons in one day in Scotland. If you complain about the weather, locals will tell you to "wait an hour".

The small towns up here will provide you with the travel essentials you'll need, so stock up before hitting the road and exploring the expansive coastline. It might also be worth bringing a decent coat and some spare footwear — there'll be a fair amount of coastal walking needed on a search to peek over the edge of cliffs for hidden nooks and crannies, and Scotland isn't known for being that dry.

Being part of the mainland UK, you can drive or take the train up to Scotland from England, or fly from domestic UK airports for cheap fares less than the cost of petrol. That said, a car or van is indispensable if you plan to explore.

SHARPY

ACCESS TO BRIMMS IS THROUGH A FARM.

SEAMUS MAKIM

BAGPIPES HANDLES BIG SWELLS WELL. IT JUST
GETS HOLLOWER AND HEAVIER! BRAD JACKSON.

ENGLAND & WALES

CULTURE, NIGHTLIFE AND BETTER WAVES THAN YOU THINK

LANGUAGE.....**ENGLISH / WELSH**
MAIN AIRPORT.....**LONDON HEATHROW**
INTERNATIONAL AIRPORT (LHR)
CURRENCY.....**BRITISH POUND STERLING**
SWELL SEASON.....**YEAR ROUND, BEST SEP-MAY**
WATER TEMP.....**6C-18C**

OUTLINE

England and Wales have a long multi-directional coastline offering a huge number and variety of breaks; open-ocean beachies, wedges, rivermouths, points, reefs and shories, all of which work on different tides, winds and swell directions. Breaks can get busy in the summer months (when the swell is smallest) but once the tourists go home and the crowds thin out, decent swell can pummel all the coastlines on this crowded island with surprising power. On their day English and Welsh bodyboarding breaks can rival anywhere in Europe, although it has to be said the really good days are few and far between! The great thing of visiting this part of the world is that there is so much to see: take in the sights of one of the world's greatest capital cities (London that is), experience the vibrant music scene, especially the summer festivals, or take in a football (soccer if you are American!) match. And if you score some good waves in between, then that's a bonus.

The county of Cornwall occupies the far south-west corner. Known as the centre of UK surfing, Cornwall is a ruggedly proud land of Celtic origin, bearing its own flag and culture. Once world-famous for its tin mining, Cornwall has since become a surf mecca, attracting a huge influx of visitors in the summer months, propping up the county's economy. The sea is blessed by the Gulf Stream, which keeps the water temperature and weather bearable although the county is on the same latitude as chilly Newfoundland.

Wales too is worth a visit, and has a thriving surf scene, centred around the stunningly beautiful Gower peninsular and the city of Swansea. Further west Pembrokeshire has some fine breaks and stunning countryside. The Welsh are a friendly bunch although very fond of the odd alcoholic beverage!

BREAKS

The southwest peninsula is the go-to region for surf in England. First stop for Londoners heading for the surf is the North Devon village of Croyde, a punchy hollow beachbreak at low tide which, due to its relative proximity to The Big Smoke, suffers

ON THEIR DAY, SOME OF CORNISH BEACHBREAKS ARE WORLD CLASS. PORTHTOWAN FIRING ON ALL CYLINDERS.

MIKE SEARLE

PORTHTOWAN, CORNWALL

A punchy and powerful beach break on Cornwall's north coast which works best on a decent W/NW swell and a SE wind. The banks at low produce solid waves which peel both left and right and can give both decent barrels and air sections. A swell magnet for the area, Porthtowan gets busy, especially in the summer, but the vibe is mellow and when long-period groundswells hit the place lights up as one of the best breaks in the county.

from crowds. Further west, Cornwall boasts a great variety of different breaks, beautiful beaches and an abundance of swell from the North Atlantic. Although wild and windy in the winter, groomed groundswells generated from US East Coast hurricanes pack a punch in the autumn, and light up hundreds of different breaks on both coasts of the county. Even the normally fairly docile beaches around Newquay like Fistral can get good at these times, and are worth a punt if you can't get a lift out to the less crowded spots.

The great thing about Cornwall is that, because of the twisted and tortured nature of its coastline, there is usually somewhere offshore (if there's swell) on any wind direction. With a high tidal range, though, a little local knowledge is extremely useful. Local spongers are a friendly bunch and

NEWQUAY NIGHTLIFE.

MIKE SEARLE

'LEVEN COMES ALIVE IN THE WINTER MONTHS, BUT
BE PREPARED TO BATTLE THE CROWDS.

MIKE SEARLE

CHRIS POWER

PORTHLEVEN, CORNWALL

One of the most renowned and respected reef breaks in the UK, the south coast spot is a short
and powerful right hand reef which will break hollow to triple overhead and beyond. It works
best on a mid tide as low gets stupidly shallow and high too backwashy. It gets crowded very
quickly on a SW swell and a sniff of NE in the wind. An alternative to the reef is the Pier
on the opposite side of the channel - best at low tide with a NE wind, the smaller, suckier
A-frame reef offers punchy short lefts into boostable bowls, and slightly longer rights which
throw hollow towards the sewage pipe. Both spots can get aggro due to small take off zones
and the sheer volume of people in the water when there's decent swell however. Although you
see surfers mixing it up with spongers on the Reef, the Pier is the sole domain of the local
boogers, who get quite tribal. However, if you show respect and let your bodyboarding do the
talking you should have a place in the lineup without too much hassle.

MIKE SEARLE

IF YOU CAN HANDLE HECTIC WEATHER YOU CAN SCORE THE SESSION OF YOUR LIFE.

TOLCARNE WEDGE, CORNWALL

THE HOME OF UK HIGH PERFORMANCE BODYBOARDING, TOLCARNE WEDGE. JAMES LEE LAUNCHES AN AIR REVERSE.

One of the best bodyboarding spots in the country, the Wedge breaks left off the west cliff of Newquay's Tolcarne Beach on larger three-quarter tides. Best on a SE wind, the cliff refracts classic side-wave wedges into the beach which ramp up, chuck out and shoot boogers down the line into oncoming bowls, perfect to boost from and clock up some air-miles. Relatively fickle, the spot doesn't handle too much swell, and only works on bigger tides. After the peak has stopped working when the tide gets too high, Seconds will usually dish up some ramps further down the beach in the shorey. Expect a tough slog to get waves when it's firing as the local boys have it dialed. When you do get one though there's a fun, fast takeoff and an almost guaranteed boost section — a booger's dream.

'THE COVE', YORKSHIRE

One of England's greatest waves, the left is a long heaving reef located on England's east cast which can reach triple overhead-plus and discharge big powerful chocolate barrels which smash down the reef in front of a picture-postcard fishing village. The lineup is usually full with a hardy local crew who charge hard, know the barrel inside out and earn their respect year-round in the cold brown water. It works best on a N/NE swell and is groomed with SSW winds.

ROHAN INGLIS PLUMBS THROUGH A CHOCOLATE BARREL ON THE UK'S EAST COAST.

MICKEY SMITH

MARTIN YELLAND

THIS SPOT IS RARELY EMPTY THESE DAYS, IF YOU SCORE IT ON YOUR OWN YOU ARE TRULY BLESSED!

are usually keen to befriend visiting bodyboarders, so a good attitude and a willingness to buy a couple of pints in the pub might result in being shown a couple of secret spots.

An eight-hour drive north of Cornwall to the east coast brings you to Yorkshire, a ruggedly beautiful county which is home to several slabbing reefs, including The Cove, a hollow left hander which holds a big swell. The downside is its location on the North Sea, which is much colder than the Gulf Stream-bathed southwest. Plus some local stand-ups can be, shall we say, a little unfriendly.

South Wales doesn't have a huge bodyboarding population, but there are some reefs dotted around the coast which fire on their day. The area doesn't pick up quite as much swell as Cornwall, but Pembrokeshire tends to be rather more consistent than other parts of the country.

BOOGVIBE

Bodyboarding is growing across the UK, especially in Cornwall, which sees the cream of the crop for waves and is the centre of the British bodyboard industry. Boog-specific shops have proliferated in recent times supporting the local scene, and Newquay is home to ThreeSixty magazine, the most respected bodyboard mag in Europe. Despite a large surfing population, there are many sponge-ruled spots around the country, which is testament to the growth of the sport and the dedicated crews who love to boog here, come rain or shine. Normally rain.

TRAVEL TIPS

Cornwall (or Kernow as it is called by those locals proud of its heritage) is a seasonal UK tourist destination which becomes busy both in sea and on land in the summer months of May to August. Expect clogged roads, crowded breaks and packed pubs during this time, but most importantly, small swell.

If you time a trip for the autumn you can ready yourself for groomed long-period groundswell, warm weather and thinning crowds. You can get away with a 3/2 summer wetsuit until October and usually won't need to don a 5/4 until the end of the year depending on your susceptibility to the cold.

Be sure to sample the famous Cornish pasty and cream teas on your trip, and indulge in the summer nightlife in Newquay when the town's population swells with thousands of holidaymakers out for a good time. Some of the sights have to be seen to be believed!

SOME OF THE BEST CORNISH SLABS AND SHOREBREAKS COME ALIVE WHEN FEROCIOUS ATLANTIC STORMS LASH THE COAST.

BOTH CORNWALL AND WALES HAVE STUNNING COASTLINES SHELTERING NUMEROUS SECRET SPOTS.

BHS,WALES

One of the best wedges in the UK, Pembrokeshire's BHS needs a solid swell to get going but delivers excellent thick wedging left handers when all the factors coincide. Taking off on the peaky sidewinder accelerates your speedscoop into the pitching section ready for some decent air time. It works best from mid tide onwards and on a NW wind, although westerlies won't ruin it completely. You'll need to get on it early to avoid crowds though, the local crew own it and will give you a BHS education when it gets good.

WELSH BODYBOARDER GARETH LATHWOOD BOOSTS A NICE INVERT AT BHS.

THE CANARY ISLANDS

IF THE VOLCANOES DON'T BLOW YOUR MIND THE BARRELS WILL

LANGUAGE.....**SPANISH**
MAIN AIRPORT.....**LAS PALMAS AIRPORT GRAN CANARIA (LPA)**
CURRENCY.....**EURO**
SWELL SEASON.....**OCT-APR**
WATER TEMP.....**18C-23C**

OUTLINE

Sixty miles off the coast of Morocco lies a group of Spanish islands which have become synonymous with high performance bodyboarding. The volcanic group consists of 13 islands, from the biggest, Tenerife (785 sq. miles), to the smallest, Isla De Lobos (1.78 sq. miles) they are blessed with year-round sunshine, mild waters and epic waves.

Dubbed the 'Atlantic Hawaii' for the quality and power of its reef breaks, these urchin-infested slabs hold some of the finest bodyboarding waves ever found, with incredibly heavy barrels and sections as thick as hydrodynamic theory allows. The islands are wave-drenched, and there are so many spots which can be world class on their day that you are never too far from a sick pit. Welcome to the Canaries.

BREAKS

The deep water drop-off surrounding the islands means swell slams the slabs with full Atlantic power, producing thick, heavy, solid waves which require 100% commitment from the second you think about pushing over the edge. What comes next depends on your ability to control your rail and work the warp or suffer the consequences. From playful 2ft punchy onshore sections to top-to-bottom monstrous quadruple-overhead towerblocks, Canarian reefs tick all the boxes. There is also a selection of less intense beachies which can be fun, although the reefs are what brings boogers the world over.

BOOGVIBE

The Canary Islands are absolutely epic, a true bodyboarding dream destination in terms of the quality and quantity of the waves on offer. The boog scene in the Canaries is huge, and spongers easily outnumber surfers at many spots. The standard of local riders is insane, and many have risen to compete at the highest level on the IBA world tour. Their style is their own, but they charge as hard as anyone, be it scooping into gargantuan bombs or boosting some of the highest aerials you will see. The flipside of the coin is that the Canaries have

MIKE SEARLE

TURN UP EARLY IF YOU WANT TO SCORE IT UNCROWDED.

EL QUEMAO

MIKE SEARLE

Lanzarote's most notorious break bears more than a passing resemblance to its Pacific brother Pipeline. El Quemao is a crunching left hand reef off the fishing village of La Santa which brought the attention of the world's surf media to Lanzarote. Offshore on the E/SE Sirocco wind, El Quemao will tear you a new one if you don't treat it with the utmost respect. A quick takeoff and perfect scoop is required to make the second section which can sometimes suck very dry. It is shallow, fast, heavy and the sharp lava reef is strewn with even sharper spined sea urchins. The locals don't take kindly to anyone, whether you rip or not. Show respect and it will improve your chances, but even then they won't welcome you with open arms. Your best bet to avoid the crowds is to try and score the early. Works best on a W/NW/N swell and easterly wind from low to mid tide.

ABOVE: EL QUEMAO CAN HOLD A DECENT SIZE. ROB BARBER SWOOPS. RIGHT: THERE ARE PLENTY OF REMOTE SECRET SPOTS IN THE CANARIES IF YOU DO SOME EXPLORATION.

become a favourite destination for many travellers, and as such tensions do rise with the locals. Although a fearsome reputation precedes them, you won't get hassle everywhere and in more instances than not their bark is worse than their bite.

CANARY ISLANDS TRAVEL TIPS

It is unfortunate to say, but aggressive localism has risen in recent years as bodyboarders and surfers the world over have come to realise the sheer potential of the Canary Islands. Crowds on the better spots are often unavoidable, so paddling out with a chilled friendly approach is easily the best option to try and neutralise any bad vibes that may be simmering. As with anywhere, show the locals respect for their waves, hoot them in, share the stoke and they will be more inclined to let you pull in and experience what the Canaries is all about. Many travellers have noticed that the locals aren't too keen to get up early, so your best bet for an empty surf is get in well before 10am.

Car crime and theft is another issue to consider, try not to leave anything of value in your car and avoid parking close to spots, especially when it's firing. Waxed windscreens, broken windows and flat tyres aren't unheard of. Surfing in groups is another way to develop a problem – seeing a crew of foreign spongers rock up and all paddle out together will do nothing but raise tensions when you make the lineup ... be considerate, travel in small groups and split sessions if needs be.

It is pretty important to keep it on the down low that you are bodyboarders when you are hiring a car too, so send in one person to hire it and keep everyone else and the bags waiting at another location. There is unfortunately almost always a need to go off road when hunting spots and even checking established ones in the Canaries. Therefore always go for the insurance option that covers you for absolutely everything, oh, and don't drink and drive – the Canarian police have that down tight. You've been warned!

The standard accommodation in the Canaries is the two-bedroom self catering apartment. Hotels are only usually well priced when you get them on a package deal (which can be worth checking out if the dates fit with your plans). The apartments will offer you a base in which to cook, chill and while

SEAMUS MAKIM

SOLOMON MOORE, ONE OF FUERTE'S BEST BODYBOARDERS.

THE BUBBLE

MIKE SEARLE

One of Fuerteventura's best boog spots, the Bubble is a sick A-frame reef on the north shore which breaks fast with hollow and pitching rights and lefts over yet another sharp, shallow reef. Deep-water swell jacks up quickly and gives good-length pits for those lucky enough to snag a wave off the locals. One of the busiest waves on the island, the locals on the peak aren't too willing to abide by general etiquette, so expect drop-ins when it's on, even if you have priority and have been quietly minding your own business for a while. Hang around, pick off a few good ones, let your bodyboarding do the talking and you will have a better chance of taking one of the well-protected set waves. The Bubble is a dream bodyboarding spot, get in early to have a better chance of avoiding the crowds. Works best on a W/NW/N swell and SE wind.

> "The Canaries is one of those places where you have to earn your respect. This is not by turning up with a van full of people on 3 foot offshore days. If you want a share I recommend going on your own and charging. Charge big and heavy waves. You'll get respect for that, then you are likely to be welcome in other conditions too."
> - Pablo Prieto

SPEWPITS

Located off the point north of Cotillo in Fuerteventura, Spewpits gives a pretty accurate description of how it delivers the goods in its name. It breaks powerfully over a shallow lava reef with sucky lefts and rights, depending on the swell direction. A swell magnet, Spewpits works best on an easterly wind when it greets its lucky visitors with beautifully groomed barrels. Prone to crowds, the reef can get very dry and is extremely happy to meet you. When big, Spewpits delivers truly world-class waves, but you'll need a good dose of manupmanship when things get hairy. Works on any SW/W/NW swell.

ALEX WILLIAMS

ANOTHER GURGLING, FAST BREAKING CANARIAN REEF BREAK. HEAVES OVER A RAZOR SHARP, URCHIN INFESTED SLAB.

THE WAVE AT CONFITAL GROWS AS
IT RUNS DOWN THE REEF, IT OFFERS
GREAT AIR AND BARREL SECTIONS.

EL CONFITAL

The best right hand barrel in the Canaries, Gran
Canaria's El Confital peels perfect makeable tubes
which rifle down the reef off the point at Casas
de las Coloradas. A previous final stop on the IBA
tour, El Confital is a long wave with bowly sections
just built for bodyboarding with a nice easy takeoff
flowing seamlessly into a fast, hollow, makeable
section. Works best on a W/NW/N swell on an E/SE
wind. Can get very crowded, but treat the locals with
respect and you may get your share.

EL FRONTON

Possibly the best bodyboarding slab in the world, El Fronton offers a loaded right
and shorter mutant left which breaks thick and fast both ways from deep water onto a
triangular ledge north of Galdar in Gran Canaria. Make no mistake, El Fronton is one
of the most serious waves regularly ridden anywhere. A super-heavy take off is quickly
met with an even heavier section wanting to swallow you whole, but if you successfully
negotiate its rumbling hunger it will burp you out into one of the thickest air ramps you
will ever have the pleasure of hitting. Rapidly gaining reputation globally as one of the
all-time greats, El Fronton has a heavy local pack as you might expect. Works best on a
NW/N/NE swell, mid to high tide and S/SE winds.

SIAM WATER PARK IN TENERIFE
HOUSES ONE OF THE BIGGEST WAVE
POOLS IN THE WORLD.

FULL ENGLISH
BREAKFAST
2 SAUSAGES
2 BACON
2 EGGS
BAKED BEANS
TOMATO & CHIPS
WITH TOASTS AND
ONLY 3.00

MIKE SEARLE

K16 IN TENERIFE IS A SUPER FUN WAVE BUT HAS
A FEARSOME REPUTATION FOR LOCALISM BUT.
REMEMBER, THE CANARIANS VERY RARELY SURF
THE EARLY, ESPECIALLY DURING CARNIVAL (RIGHT).

away the hours reading/playing cards/
Facebooking until the wind calms down
for the evening session.

These days with the more accurate
surf prediction forecasting websites,
you would expect to be able to plan a
night out before a day with a poor surf
forecast, but the Atlantic islands are a
law unto themselves, with swell and
wind rarely behaving how the forecast
suggests they will. In the last weeks of
February and early March the Canarian
carnival travels from island to island
and is something that once you have
experienced you will want to check
out again and again. The whole of the
island spends the night (or a couple of
days and nights in many cases) partying
Latino style.

The islands are capable of

hoovering swell from almost all
directions, but most big swells come
from the slow-moving North Atlantic
lows which churn out groundswell
striking the islands from the north west.
US East Coast hurricane swell can also
reach the island chain if storms peel
away from the continent early and don't
dissipate too soon. Predominant trade
winds blow year-round from the north
east, but are lighter in October and
November. Cheap flights can be picked
up online from mainland Europe, with
the most popular airports being two
(TFN and TFS) in Tenerife, and the main
Gran Canaria Airport (LPA). Visas are not
required for British, Australian, Canadian,
EU, Japanese and USA visitors, but
return tickets are.

"El Fronton is a super-heavy right and left slab reef
break and quite simply one of the best bodyboard
waves in the world." - Jeff Hubbard

"It gives you a chance to go to the moon on the
right section...a right and left peak that has limitless
possibilities on a bodyboard." - Michael Novy

RUBEN REDONDO, EL FRONTON.

MOROCCO

THE DUSTY CORNER OF NORTH WEST AFRICA HAS A LITTLE SECRET

LANGUAGE.....**ARABIC AND FRENCH**
MAIN AIRPORT.....**AGADIR AL MASSIRA AIRPORT (AGA)**
CURRENCY.....**MOROCCAN DIRHAM**
SWELL SEASON.....**OCT-APR**
WATER TEMP.....**16C-25C**

OUTLINE

Occupying the Atlantic-facing north west corner of Africa, Morocco is a swell-soaked Arabic country with some of the best point breaks in the world. Lazily sprawling between the pulsing green Atlantic and the rich red hues of Saharan sands, Morocco's surfing coastline stretches from the Strait of Gilbraltar all the way south to its border with Western Sahara. Morocco is home to the Atlas and Rif mountain ranges and an almost exclusive Arab-Berber population.

A long-time staple of the travelling surfers, Morocco has recently seen a steady increase in travelling European bodyboarders looking for an alternative winter destination. Cheap flights, affordable accommodation and a sick variety of waves keeps those boogers in the know coming back for more year after year.

BREAKS

It is a common misconception that Moroccan waves consist of nothing more than a multitude of big fat right-hand point breaks. Yes, it is true the quality of the points does favour stand-ups, but Morocco has many other types of break which more than tip the balance back in favour of the boogers.

The former desert fishing village of Taghazoute and its reeling points in the south was the place that was first colonised by surfers in the 70s, when there was no running water or electricity. These days there are plenty of home comforts and a good selection of places to stay, from cheap dives to smart apartments and surf

REDA WAVE HUNTER

CASCADES

Located in front of the surf club at Rabat, Cascades is a wedgy left and right A-frame reef just made for bodyboarding and gives you a fast drop, quick scoop and pitching lip to boost straight out of. Due to its location close to town (and the frothing pack of local boogers that have it wired) it can get crowded, but the standard of local riding is something to behold. It needs SE winds to be clean and breaks on a mere sniff of swell, so can max out quickly if the buoys are up.

MOROCCO IS FAMED FOR ITS REELING
RIGHTHAND POINT BREAKS BUT THERE
IS MORE TO IT THAN JUST FAT SURFERS'
WAVES. WHEN THE SWELL IS RUNNING YOU
WILL BE VERY SURPRISED BY THE AMOUNT
OF AMAZING BODYBOARDING WAVES.

TAGHAZOUTE REEFS & WEDGES

Taghazoute Wedges - The surfing gateway to the south, Taghazoute is home to the famous points of Killers, Boilers and Anchors, but also holds some of the best wedges in the country. Both right and left hand peaks can be found nestled in the nooks and crannies of the sweeping headlands and jagged coves not 20 minutes from Taghazoute in either direction. The wedges work best on E/NE winds and a sizey swell that wraps beyond the points and into where the fun starts.

Taghazoute Reefs - While most travellers in the region check out the more renowned spots which are guaranteed on big swells to be heaving (both in size and crowds) there are some absolutely sick left and right reefs in the Taghazoute area. Varying from fun chuckable barrels and shoulders to intense slabs, search carefully and ye shall most definitely find.

camps. Only 30 minutes drive from the airport at Agadir, it's a good base for exploring some of the wedges and reefs in the neighbourhood.

About 600km (375 miles) north up the coast, the city of Rabat is the place to base yourself to sample the reefs at Cascades and Sharatan. Fly into Casablanca or Marrakech and get the superb train through the desert. A first class ticket costs about the $18 US.

The long grinding barrels of Safi are about halfway between Rabat and Agadir. Desert wedges, reefs and beachies are spread copiously along hundreds of miles of rugged and crumbly coastline, which just so happens to closely mirror the dusty highway; so jump in to a hire car, buckle up, and drive, this coast will reward some serious exploration.

BOOGVIBE

Pierre Louis Costes took up the sport when living in Morocco as a grom and local riders like Brahim Idouch and Adrane Benslimane seem determined to shred like him, boosting big moves on anything going. Although this is a relatively poor country and most groms can't afford to bodyboard, government funding is available for competitive bodyboarding and Moroccan riders are doing well on the European tour. The scene in Morocco has gone from strength to strength in the last decade, and the general vibe is mellow from Moroccans; you are more likely to get dropped in on by mainland European surfers who are simply over-frothing because they usually surf river waves or are amazed at their new-found ability to paddle in to a wave and stand up on their board!

ONE OF THE LOW KEY WEDGE WAVES THAT ARE DOTTED AROUND THE TAGHAZOUTE AREA.

SHARATAN

A miniature Mundaka in the town of Mehdya about a 30 minute drive north of Rabat. It breaks over a reef bottom up an extended river mouth framed by two breakwalls. It needs a big swell to give a wedgy ramp off the rocks into a no-holds-barred tube ride which reels and reels and can handle 8ft plus. Quite protected from most winds but straight west, it needs an east to groom the lip and keep it peeling. Getting in and out can be a little sketchy due to the boulders on the shoreline, but it is one of the best boog waves on the whole stretch, and, bizarrely, in a river.

BROOKE MASON CLOCKS UP SOME TUBE TIME AT A SECRET SOUTHERN MOROCCO SLAB.

SAFI

Further up the coast in Central Morocco, Safi is a point break with a difference — it is hollow. Needs a big swell to get going, but Safi can barrel — barrel — for half a kilometer straight. That's top-to-bottom triple overhead barrels, reminiscent of Kirra or a right-hand Mundaka. Safi needs a a big swell to break, which tends to be when the big winter storms in the northern Atlantic generate long-fetch waves. Safi does have a dedicated local crew so be respectful or expect to face some hostility. The fact you bodyboard may work in your favour if you are totally outnumbered - just make sure you abide by the pecking order and when you do go for one, make it stick. Works best at low to mid tide, Safi is a world-class monster which many claim to be the best wave in the country.

ANCHOR POINT

One of the best point breaks in the world when there's a big swell, Anchors is just north of Taghazoute. So called because apparently there used to be an anchor factory on the point, the ruins of which provide an atmospheric backdrop to the action in the water. Offshore on NE to E wind, it holds a big swell and works throughout the tide, but is wally at mid to high, great if you are looking for big long faces to carve on, but not much else. It can run for a couple of hundred metres and gets crowded when it is smaller. At low tide however, the inside section transforms itself into a super fun bodyboarding wave with a fast down-the-line barrel. Beware of the strong sweep down the point when it's over 4ft. There are several other fun breaks within walking distance of Anchors which work at different tides. Well worth a bit of exploration.

ANCHOR POINT CAN BE A SUPER FUN BODYBOARDING WAVE ON THE RIGHT TIDE AND WIND DIRECTION.

AARON DINHAM PUNTS AN INVERT AT ONE OF TAGHAZOUTE'S SECRET WEDGES.

RICARDO BORGHI

SAFI IS THE BEST WAVE IN MOROCCO, IF YOU ARE LUCKY ENOUGH TO SCORE IT YOU WILL NEVER FORGET IT. AIDAN SALMON GETTING SHACKED OUT OF HIS MIND!

MOROCCO TRAVEL TIPS

Localism isn't really an issue in the water, the only hiccup you might encounter is if you stumble across a secret spot and park your car close by. With thousands of travelling surfers descending on the parched wave-rich coast every winter, you can't blame local Moroccans for wanting to keep their secrets to themselves. Likewise, if you spot a few cars hastily parked behind bushes and cacti off the side of the road you may have been alerted to a spot for another day.

Morocco is a developing country. Litter, poor hygiene and iffy sanitation go hand in hand with travelling here, especially in the cities. But the people are very friendly and happy to meet you, and a little French lingo will help you get by. The marketplaces are buzzing hives of colour, scent and flavour. A trip to the ancient city of Marrakech is a must if you have time.

Moroccan food is delicious, and local 'Berber whisky' (sweet mint green tea) is consumed by the bucket load. As

Morocco is an Islamic state, alcohol is a bit of a grey area; it is available from some shops but it should be consumed in the privacy of your accommodation. Likewise, street vendors will offer you cheap bags of h*ashish* (marijuana). Beware, the police do turn a blind eye to the locals' consumption, but you won't be so favourably treated if they catch you in possession.

Morocco is a monarchy and although the king has gone a long way to try to modernise the country, you will see many women wearing the *hijab* or headscarf (although it is not a strict Islamic nation).

As a major tourist destination Marrakech has a good selection of incoming flights from budget airlines, and gives good access to the north and south. Casablanca in the north and Agadir in the south are alternative airports. Moroccan currency is the dirham, which you are unable to buy until you enter the country. ATMs are fairly plentiful in the main towns and cities though.

MIKE SEARLE

In Search of African Gold

By Owen Pye

THE TROUBLE WITH DECLARING YOU ARE A JOURNALIST (AND HAVING A PASSPORT PHOTO THAT FOR SOME REASON LOOKS LIKE YOU ARE A 65-YEAR-OLD MEMBER OF THE TALIBAN) IS THAT IMMIGRATION OFFICIALS OFTEN FIND YOU OBJECTIONABLE.

After several minutes of trying to explain to the man behind the impeccable moustache that the reason he hadn't heard of the newspaper I worked for was because it wasn't circulated in Agadir, we strolled out and loaded up the vans to brave the carnage of the Moroccan highways.

I was still half-asleep as we arrived at Onze, a finger of reef offering up some tasty lefts and rights through the early morning mist. We paddled out, somewhat wary of the massive Saudi Arabian property further down the beach. The huge walled compound, given to a Saudi prince by the Moroccan king, actually has armed guards stationed at it ready to fire warning shots if you drift too far down towards it. With that in mind, we took the lefts.

The following days consisted of alternating between the heavy beachie of Tifnit in the south and the consistent reefs and wedges around Taghazoute,

tucked away and totally rippable. The stoke had been high, both in the water and in the cactus fields above, where we stashed our dusty hire cars out of view from the passing highway and where the local kids gathered to watch the show.

Towards the end of the trip we found the sickest wave to date found in Morocco. A shallow and fast right-hand slab, its location is top secret and we needed to bro-down with the local sponge crew to avoid being attacked by a local surf guide for even parking near to it. Trip grom Lloyd wasn't having a good day. "I got offered drugs again, hit my head on the car door three times whilst getting changed, almost got mugged, then a bird sh*t on me." How could it get any worse? He guarded the car on a deserted clifftop whilst we checked the slab. When we came back we found he had been offered a blow job by a local chap for 100 dirham. That's $10US. It really wasn't his day.

We came to this country unsure of just how good it could be for high performance bodyboarding, but we all left with a knowing smile. The standard of riding here by local boogers is excellent, not just for the level of tweak, but for the sections they bust off doing them. They are able to make a crappy one foot mushburger shorey look as boostable as 6ft Fronton.

Yes you dodge maniacal moped riders, seemingly drunk truck drivers and meandering pedestrians each time you want to go anywhere, but that's part of the Moroccan thrill. From empty desert points to bustling marketplaces, the fabric of its society — accompanied by a great deal of litter and stray animals — well, just somehow works.

Although the country is poor, a real richness can come in experiences for the untamed traveller. We only searched a small section of the beautifully parched coastline of Morocco, but with more time, an open mind and a taste for adventure, the potential for bodyboarding here is nothing short of epic.

ONE OF THE TOP MOROCCAN
SHREDDERS, YASSINE IDDOUCH

SOUTH AFRICA

TWO OCEANS, QUALITY WAVES GALORE

LANGUAGE.....**ENGLISH /AFRIKAANS / NDEBELE / NORTHERN SOTHO /
SOUTHERN SOTHO / SWAZI / TSONGA / TSWANA /VENDA / XHOSA / ZULU**
MAIN AIRPORT.....**DURBAN INTERNATIONAL AIRPORT (DUR)**
CURRENCY.....**SOUTH AFRICAN RAND**
SWELL SEASON.....**YEAR ROUND, BEST MAR-SEP**
WATER TEMP.....**14C-22C**

OUTLINE

South Africa occupies the toe of the continent with 1,739 miles of coastline facing west, south and east. Right in the path of the strong westerly winds of the Roaring Forties, South Africa straddles the South Atlantic and Indian Oceans and holds some of the wildest, heaviest and most coveted waves in the world.

Whether you are talking about its geography, history, environment, people, economy, culture, history or politics, the one word more apt than any other to describe South Africa would be diverse. This also encompasses its rich marine life, which flourishes in the mix of cold and warm waters and does include the infamous great white. The risk of attack is always a talking point for surfers travelling to South Africa, even though the likelihood is very small.

If you arrive in Cape Town in September, you owe yourself a visit to the west coast and the wildflower areas. Here you can witness one of the most spectacular natural events in the country as thousands of square kilometres of land becomes carpeted with colourful flowers. Table Mountain offers majestic views over the city, the Atlantic Seaboard, and Robben Island - a World Heritage Site and museum where Nelson Mandela spent 27 years in prison for his role in fighting apartheid.

Cape Town has a rich blend of cultures and nationalities. With pristine turquoise waters and spotless white sand beaches, Cape Town has become a Mecca for ambitious travellers looking to experience their own slice of paradise. The cosmopolitan city also attracts beautiful people from around the globe, driving its modeling industry from November to April and rubbing shoulders with the rich and famous.

BREAKS

There is such variety in South African spots an adventurous trip will see you encounter all types, from warm and friendly netted beachies and punchy wedges to distant heaving reefs and wild cold-water slabs you'd need an unhealthy blend of courage and insanity to tackle. Away from the surf city culture of Durban in the east, the South African coastline gets wild.

Spend enough time in the Cape Town area and you'll be sure to find top boogers Jared Houston, Sacha Specker and the brothers Josh and Aden Kleve ripping it up with Saffa power. There are four standout spots in Cape Town. 3de Steen is a peaky beachie on the west coast. Llandudno is a heavily localised wedgy righthander near the city. In the Kommetjie area there are numerous spots on the South Peninsula that work on a variety of conditions. Finally Kalk Bay is a lefthand slab that works on opposing conditions to the other spots. This place is usually crowded and localised, but you can get some beauties here during the week when the working folk are off doing their thing.

Although ambient summer temperatures stay between 26-38ºC (79ºF-100ºF), the water drops to a frigid 9-14ºC (48ºF-57ºF) as the summer offshores create massive upwelling, stirring the icy deep ocean water to the surface. This upwelling supports some of the richest sealife on the planet, keeping a healthy population of great white sharks feeding on Cape fur seals. While great whites are often seen in the waters off Cape Town, attacks on humans are rare.

PLETT WEDGE CAN BE AMAZING FUN BETWEEN THREE AND FIVE FOOT.

SIMON HEALE

PLETTENBERG WEDGE

An hour west of J-Bay, Plettenberg Wedge breaks in front of the town on easterly swells which the rocks on the little headland and offer up a left-hand bodyboarding nirvana with rampy tak long walling wedges to smash. It can get very hollow and thumping kegs can be mixed up with s sections when the factors all align. Sand bottomed, it breaks close to shore and works best w on a west wind. If there is too much south in the swell to make the wedge work (or the crowds too much) there are many other spots in the area which will break, so all is not lost.

ALAN VAN GYSEN

"Cave Rock is a really good reef break that works best in the winter time from April to July. It's probably one of the best waves on the east coast of South Africa, it's a technical wave that doesn't get surfed too much over four foot, it's a really good high performance wave." – Mark McCarthy

SCOTTBURGH PIPE

A fun, hollow right-hander which breaks over a sand and rock bottom in front of the caravan park at Scottburgh, around 45 minutes south of Durban. Scottburgh Pipe picks up a fair bit of swell and can give very good barrels. It is considered one of the better bodyboarding waves in the area, and although it does work on a mid-size swell it needs to be fairly big to come into its own. Works best on S/SE swells and W/NW winds.

ALAN VAN GYSEN

CAVE ROCK

One of the heaviest spots in Durban, Cave Rock is a serious right hand reef which can hold massive swell and detonates big barrels under powerful lips which guillotine down its reef at speed. The Rock is thick, hollow and intense. It requires full commitment when big, but negotiate the scoop successfully and a spat reward here is a keeper. To get there aim for Brighton Beach in south Durban and if it's going off you won't miss it. Very consistent, and works best on a NW wind.

NORTH BEACH

Durban is South Africa's "surf city" and its main beach, North, has
for a long time been SA bodyboarding's epicentre. North Beach is
a peaky right beachie that can handle decent swell and give hollow
waves with punchy sections. Fun when small but better when big,
North Beach works best on a big southeast swell with light offshore
west winds. According to Mark McCarthy this is when you can get
the biggest right hand barrels. Being a city beach it can get very
crowded (especially at the weekend or when there is swell).

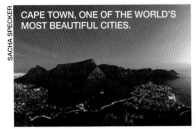
SACHA SPECKER

CAPE TOWN, ONE OF THE WORLD'S MOST BEAUTIFUL CITIES.

SACHA SPECKER

GREG FRASIER ENJOYING A JACK STANCE PIT AT THE HOEK IN CAPE TOWN.

ALAN VAN GYSEN

JARED HOUSTON BOTTOM TURNS ON A DEVIL'S HORN BOMB

SACHA SPECKER

CAPE TOWN SLAB.

SOUTH AFRICA TRAVEL TIPS

Be sure to check out SA's pristine game reserves and stunning national parks – there can't be too many other surf destinations where you'll find roaming lion, rhino, leopard, buffalo and elephant a few hours from the waves. Likewise if you are in Durban with time to kill make a point to head to the Wave House, it is the biggest man-made stationary wave in the world and capable of delivering overhead barrels and hilarious beatdowns.

South Africa is an extremely consistent surf destination, and its east coast swell is groomed with blessed light offshores in the winter months. This coincides with one of the biggest migrations on earth — that of the sardines, which move up the east coast in a giant shoal to find warmer waters. Although a beautiful phenomenon, it does bring a feeding frenzy to those higher up the food chain, including sharks. Although Durban hasn't had a fatal shark attack since it netted its beaches in 1962, breaks further afield don't have this luxury so caution should be exercised. Although most shark attacks are thought to be cases of 'mistaken

identity', it is advisable not to surf at dawn, dusk, or in murky waters after river run off.

Sadly, serious crime is an unfortunate part of life in South Africa, especially in certain districts and suburbs. Most cases of violent crime occur in the townships but the South African authorities give high priority to protecting tourists, so tourist areas tend to be safer. The obvious advice is to be sensible when heading out, especially in the evenings. Stick with friends and be low key, don't walk around with an expensive camera around your neck and gold watch on display. The townships suffer from abject poverty, and advertising the fact you are carrying expensive items is asking for trouble. If you are held up in these areas it is advisable to give up what you have immediately and not try and fight.

Currency is in rand, and residents from many developed countries don't require a visa for stays of up to 90 days. Make sure you have at least two empty pages in your passport before you set off, or you may be turned back on arrival.

BOOGVIBE

South Africans are bodyboard mad and there is a huge push to get young groms competing to become the next Andre Botha, Mark McCarthy or Jared Houston. The competition scene is strong, and Saffas charge hard, very much reflecting the waves they have on tap. There isn't too much heavy localism in SA, but expect there to be established pecking orders on the best spots, especially in and around Durban. Be sensible, show respect, and you'll find Saffa boogers a friendly enough bunch.

PHILIPPINES

HOME TO SOME OF THE MOST PERFECT YET FICKLE WAVES EVER DISCOVERED

LANGUAGE.....**FILIPINO**
MAIN AIRPORT.....**MACTAN-CEBU INTERNATIONAL AIRPORT (CEB)**
CURRENCY.....**PHILIPPINE PESO**
SWELL SEASON.....**OCT-JAN**
WATER TEMP.....**23C-31C**

OUTLINE

The Philippines has been compared to Indonesia in the 1970s for the quality of its tropical reef breaks, many of which remain undiscovered. Located between Taiwan and Indonesia, the main island has a number of excellent breaks, although for those travelling spongers who want a proper adventure, untold new spots are ready to be found. When you consider the Philippines has 7,107 islands, almost every trip along its eastern fringes will offer up hidden gold — how much of it you can plunder depends on your willingness to disappear from civilisation.

Despite the sick setups that wait on the edges of its deep jungle, the Philippines is prone to inconsistency and can be very fickle, expect to wait months for waves if you come off-season. East Asian typhoons generate groundswell which makes August to November the best time to visit.

One of the last remaining bastions of proper surf exploration, the Philippines comes with its fair share of dangers, including malaria, tropical infections and political instability.

BREAKS

Siargao Island is the fabled destination of the Philippines thanks to the jewel in its crown; Cloud 9. The fast right hander is world class when there is swell, but is seasonal and can be fickle. There are a number of other great breaks nearby if the crowds get to be an issue, but many will require boat rides to get to – fortunately these can be had for cheap. Accommodation is also inexpensive, the food fresh, and the waters as clear and warm as a bath. There is no known malaria on Siargao, although mozzies are still ever-present. The Pacific deep water trench just offshore means groundswell hits with power.

BOOGVIBE

There isn't a huge bodyboarding scene in the Philippines but you are almost guaranteed to meet fellow travelling boogers from all corners of the world. Many of the more crowded spots will also host foreign surfers on world trips or local kids on previously snapped shortboards held together with staples. Your equipment needs to be up to the task as finding

IF YOU GET IT ON, THE PHILIPPINES HAVE SOME
OF THE WORLDS MOST FLAWLESS WAVES.
CLOUD 9 - MECHANICAL PERFECTION.

CLOUD 9

A fast and perfect barrelling right hand reef (with shorter left) in front of the famous rickety wooden platform and viewing tower. The wave is shallow and throws quickly but even your gran could get barrelled here. SW winds are offshore, and as with most of the spots in the Philippines, works best off NE typhoon groundswell. Higher tides are more friendly. The fame, international competitions and notoriety of Cloud 9 has led to it rightfully developing the nickname of Crowd 9. No-one knows the reef better than the packs of local groms, who rip from deep in the barrel on battered old boards left behind from travelling surfers. Be patient, show respect, and you'll be sure to reap the benefits.

VICTOR GONZALEZ GARCIA

AITOR ROMO ON CLOUD 9.

"Cloud 9 is one place that the brochures do actually capture the paradise that it is. The wave itself offers no boundaries, you can sit and wait for the ones that barrel the whole length of the reef, or pick off the short ones with massive ramps. Cloud 9 has it all, at six foot it's the most perfect wave for a bodyboard." — Matt Lackey

STIMPY'S

A heavy and critical left which wraps in around a barrier island and breaks onto a shallow reef. A fast and warpy barrel, it needs full commitment from take off on the bigger days. More susceptible to changing winds, it offers waves from long walling sections to thick pits. It works best on a NW wind and a swell with a little more east in it, as it wraps around the island. Share a boat from any of the Cloud 9 resorts.

TUASON POINT

An alternative to Cloud 9 if the crowds are hectic and considered as the best left on the island, Tuason Point is just around the corner to the south and picks up most swell going (which is good considering there can be long periods of small swell in the Philippines.) A powerful wave when over head high, get it early in the morning when it's glassy and hold on tight, it gets heavy. Works best on high tide with a westerly wind.

THE SWELL MAGNET THAT IS TUASON POINT.

WITH LOVELY WARM WATER, CHEAP LIVING AND A TROPICAL BACK DROP, THE PHILIPPINES CAN BE THE DREAM TRIP.

G1

A lesser-surfed A-frame reef that breaks behind Daku Island, a couple of miles south of Cloud 9 and Tuason Point. A short, fast and barrelling peak, it breaks both ways over live coral and is extremely shallow at low tide. Gives short but fun hollow tubes, but can remain dormant for long periods when the swell is small. Works best on a larger E/NE swell with westerly winds. Ask a boat to take you out beyond Daku Island, which is 10-15 minutes across the lagoon from General Luna. Also known under the name of Paradise.

ROCK ISLAND

A long right hander that gets good when the swell is NE and the wind from the west. It works throughout the tide but can suffer more in switching winds being located 3km offshore. You'll need to hire a boat to get to it, so go with a few others to lower your cost. Located a few kilometres north of Cloud 9, it's a longer, less mental right-hand version of Stimpy's, a couple of clicks further up the reef.

replacements is unlikely, and when there is swell the waves are powerful, fast and hollow. Many spots break over sharp coral at shallow depths, so expect to lose skin at some point in your trip – bring a basic first aid kit. As bodyboarders will be in the minority, expect a bit more interest by locals for tackling the waves on a sponge – many local kids will expect you to be a pro. Be friendly and generous and you will have just as many waves as anyone else.

PHILIPPINES TRAVEL TIPS

The Philippines is a beautiful unexplored archipelago of islands, home to many world class waves – some found, many not. The vast majority of people are very poor, many towns and cities are poverty-stricken, and some of the more isolated villages will be staggered to see foreigners...let alone ones carrying bodyboard bags. Be kind and generous to the flocks of kids that will run out to meet you and bombard you with smiles and shouts.

One of the massive draws of Siargao is the cost of your stay – beds can be had from as little as $16 (USD) a night for a beachfront pad. The closer you get to Cloud 9 the costs rise, but then you lower your transport costs to and from the waves. Bearing in mind it is literally paradise here, the cost of your stay is excellent value.

Temperatures are tropical, and vary from 21°C to 32°C (70°F to 90°F) depending on the season, the average annual air temperature is 27°C (80°F). Thunderstorms and typhoons are active from July to October, expect big rains and possible flooding. The climate is generally dry from December to May. The water temperature is a boardshorts-consistent 27°C – 29°C (80°F to 84°F).

It's worth bringing a couple of boards and leashes. There isn't a bodyboard market here, and your equipment needs to be up to the task as finding replacements is unlikely. Due to the warm water a firm PP board is recommended, with at least one stringer. Most waves are steep and hollow, so speed is much less of an issue than holding a rail. Crescent tail with channels is recommended, with 60/40 or even 50/50 rails for some slabbier spots.

When there is swell the waves are powerful, fast and hollow. Many spots break over sharp coral at shallow depths, so expect to lose skin at some point in your trip.

Take some time out to snorkel, dive and explore the little limestone islands on boat trips – you will see some incredible sights, and the water clarity is superb with huge schools of colourful fish.

Make sure you have comprehensive travel insurance, all your jabs, malaria tablets and six months left on your passport before it expires, with an exit journey booked. Filipino tourist visas are not required for stays of up to 21 days, but you can extend this to 90 days on a single-entry for $101 (US). Considering the likelihood of swell inconsistency, this is recommended.

Leave enough time to stay here a while — be patient, ready to explore, suck up your fear of big insects, and prepare to have your eyes opened, it is a beautiful place with beautiful waves.

VICTOR GONZÁLEZ GARCÍA

PICK YOUR WAY ACROSS THE REEF THEN SPEND YOUR SESSION HANGING OUT IN THE BARREL!

MICKEY SMITH

BATTERED, BRUISED, HIGH ON PAINKILLERS AND $2000 DOLLARS POORER, DANNY WALL SLOTS INTO THE KIND OF WAVE YOU CAN PROUDLY TELL YOUR GRANDCHILDREN ABOUT.

Russian roulette: a last-minute mission to macking Chopes

By Mickey Smith

IT WAS EARLY AUGUST, AND THE BUZZ ON THE NET WAS THAT A MASSIVE PACIFIC SWELL WAS DUE TO HIT TAHITI IN A FEW DAYS' TIME.

The forecast looked amazing, the best it had been all season. I was on the other side of the world, in Ireland, and I knew the cost of a last-minute plane ticket would be horrendous. But one way or another I had to get myself over there.

There was only one person in the UK who'd be mad enough to join me on a stupidly risky mission like this. The one and only Daniel J Wall. Thankfully, all it took to get him amped was the mention of booming 10-foot waves at Teahupoo.

"It's lookin' like the swell of the season, pard. You up for it?"

"Yeah, could well be, mate. How much are tickets?"

"Well, erm...the cheapest I've found so far is £1,500."

Wall almost choked up his breakfast. "ARE YOU HAVIN' A F--KIN' LAUGH?! Bloody hell. Well, if you can get one for 1,300 quid I'll do it. Let me know. Alright Smith, cheers."

Four hours later, after some frantic phone calls and much haggling, I found a travel agent offering round the world tickets for £1,300 each (about $2000 US). By 9am the next morning we were checked in at Bristol, bound for our first stop – New York.

We arrived in the Big Shmoke with a whole evening to kill so we hooked up with a mate of mine, Chuck Guarino, who runs super-fly clothing label Plastic People. Chuck took us to some rad little bars and we sampled a few beers. By midnight we were all pretty leathered and

I headed back to Chuck's pad to crash on his sofa. Wall meanwhile hit the town, clearly lovin' the freedom of being off the domestic leash. When I woke up at 8am I discovered I had about 10 missed calls from my travel companion, who'd ended up stumbling all the way across the Brooklyn Bridge, without a clue how to get back!

After an expensive taxi ride to pick up Wall and get to JFK, we were on our way again. God knows how Wall was feeling after no sleep; I was already on my last legs. And in a few hours we'd be dealing with 10-foot Chopes. Interesting.

We arrived in Tahiti at 2am local time, and by the time we'd blagged a lift and made our way to the village at Teahupoo it was already time to get organised and out into the lineup. At the house where we were staying, the Aussie boys were up early, stretching and preparing their gear. God knows what they thought when they saw me and Wall staggering in like a pair of junkies from a skag den!

We grabbed a baguette each from Mr Miagi's bread van, and Wall puffed his way through about 30 cigarettes. An hour later we were out the back at Chopes. The lineup was crowded and the swell was rising fast.

As usually happens when travelling with Mr Wall, it didn't take long for carnage to ensue. On his second wave he had to bail to avoid a hectic collision and freefell to his doom. He eventually came up in the lagoon, pointing to the shore and grimacing in pain. A close inspection of the damage revealed a tiger clawed arm and a massively bruised (already purple!) right thigh muscle. Two waves down and already injured, Wall sat and chain-smoked another 30 Marlboro while contemplating his predicament. It looked ominously as though he'd just blown the swell of the

year, and a £1,300 airfare.

The next morning Wall woke up with virtually no movement in his leg. But that wasn't gonna stop the ol' bulldog. Having necked five times the recommended dose of some dodgy Indo painkillers, he paddled out to what was by then massive Chopes, looking as dizzy as a daisy in a psychedelic rave flick.

The swell was pumping now – massive barrels were unloading on the reef and the bodyboarders were absolutely havin' it. Wall wasn't exactly firing on all cylinders but he got a few good ones, including a wrapping west bomb that no-one else even wanted to look at.

The swell continued to build and after a couple of hours the tow-in crew were on it, taking most of the best set waves. Only Brendo, Skipp, Eddie Soloman and Ross McBride were left paddling into random bombs, ducking under tow ropes and 15-footers, oh joy! I cruised in the water shooting photos, dodging west bombs and watching some of the best tube riding I've ever witnessed, it was absolutely insane.

The lineup was rammed the next morning so me and Wall sat it out until the arvo. Around lunchtime people started coming in, even though the waves were still absolutely pumping at a solid 10 feet.

Wall was dosed up again, but this time around he got his wave selection wired and nailed a few sweet tubes. By now consistent sets were pulsing through, and before long the arvo session turned into a dream session with only us and a few Aussies out, plus Laird Hamilton and Mark Healey towing.

After about an hour, a super hectic set wave loomed up out of nowhere. This thing was nuts, and was growing even bigger down the line. In true Wall

style, the boy from Blighty spun late, put his head down and went for it. As he shot past me in the barrel I remember thinking, "That was fricking nuts! There's no way he's coming out of that!"

Pushing through the wave, I surfaced and looked up to see the next wave. I think I let out a little whimper. It was one of the biggest west bowls to come in throughout the entire swell and it was draining all its weight into such a heavy lump of water that I was left scratching for my life to get under it. Eventually I popped up out the back. But where was Wall? I couldn't see him anywhere.

Lairdy boy burned over on his ski and said, "Hey, I think you'd better look out for your friend. That was so heavy!"

To everyone's relief, Wall surfaced in the lagoon and pointed to the shore with a grin. Later he ran me through what had happened: "After I went past you on that first one I saw the lip throwing miles down the line and I started thinking, 'I might be in trouble here!' The shockwave nailed me and I did about six cartwheels in the barrel before I even went underwater. When I came up I saw the next wave and I pretty much had a heart attack. I didn't even bother swimming under it, I just got smashed. I was moving so fast underwater...if I'd hit the bottom that would've been it. F--kin' right laugh!"

That was Wall's last day, and although he'd only had a handful of sessions at Chopes, he'd got what he came for. He'd seen Chopes as big as it gets, scored some massive barrels, and escaped with all his limbs intact. While I stayed on for another week, he flew back solo...and was back at work on the building site the following Monday morning. I got a text from him a few days later: "Nice one, Mick. Best two grand I ever spent."

INDONESIA

SO MANY WAVES, SO LITTLE TIME

LANGUAGE.....**INDONESIAN**
MAIN AIRPORT.....**DENPASAR INTERNATIONAL AIRPORT, BALI (DPS)**
CURRENCY.....**INDONESIAN RUPIAH**
SWELL SEASON.....**YEAR ROUND, BEST APR-OCT**
WATER TEMP.....**26C-31C**

ALAN VANGYSEN

PERFECT SPINNING BARREL,
AFTER PERFECT SPINNING BARREL,
MACARONI'S IS A DREAM WAVE.

OUTLINE

The country of Indonesia is located between Australia and South East Asia and consists of more than 13,000 islands. Such is the vastness of the world's biggest archipelago this is just an official estimate – even the government isn't completely certain how many there are! With only 6,000 islands inhabited, it leaves a staggering number (roughly the same as the entire number of islands in the Philippines) which remain uninhabited...so the potential for surf exploration is mind boggling.

Indonesia is a paradise in every sense of the word. World-class waves, bath-warm water, tropical climate, rich history and environment, unique biodiversity, varying cultures, ethnicities and peoples, cheap living, great food, and a staggering swell consistency. The question isn't whether you should go to Indonesia, it's for how long. With so many islands receiving surf, you could truly spend a lifetime searching the archipelago's distant islands for the perfect wave ... and, amazingly, you'd be guaranteed to find more than you'd be able to remember.

BREAKS

Indonesia is revered as the home of the perfect warm-water barrel. A distant swell-pumping machine, Antarctic storms generate almost non-stop corduroy lines out of the south Indian Ocean from April to October, quietly travelling for thousands of miles before striking the pristine reefs of Bali, Lombok, Sumbawa, Java, Sumatra and the Mentawais. Holding some of the finest waves ever surfed, these islands have naturally become popular destinations for travelling bodyboarders, but with a little adventurous spirit uncrowded perfection is still very attainable.

MACARONIS, MENTAWAIS ISLANDS

One of the most fun waves you will ever boog, Macaronis is a world-class left hand reef which wraps off a little headland in the southern Mentawais. Giving mechanical tubes, smackable lips, hollow sections and big shoulders to throw buckets off, Macaronis is the perfect playground to hone every trick in your bag. Best at mid tide, a healthy SW swell and east winds, its reputation has naturally led to increasing numbers of charter-boat-trip-foreign-standups crowding the lineup during May to October. Still, if you can be patient enough to jostle and scoop into one, you'll be an instant Maccas convert — crowd or no crowd.

THE WEDGING LEFTS OF ULU'S OFFER AMAZING RAMPS FOR TRAVELLING BODYBOARDERS. THE CROWD THESE DAYS IS THE ONLY NEGATIVE, BUT IF YOU GO TO BALI, YOU HAVE TO SURF ULUWATU. ROB BARBER BUSTS A FLIP OUT OF THE INSIDE BOWL.

"Having been to Indo a number of times in the past decade, I can say it has not changed one bit. Yes, the streets are more crowded, the waves are more crowded, the Balinese hassle you more than ever and the Western World has definitely had its impact but there are still countless hidden treasures where you and your mates can score the best waves you have ever dreamed of for weeks on end without seeing another white skin!"- Sacha Specker

ULUWATU, BALI

The Balinese swell magnet sits on the end of the Bukit Peninsula beyond the famous cave and picks up anything going, working on very small swell all the way up to 12ft-plus. Consists of a number of lefthand peaks spread down the reef, the furthest out being Temples, which has a greater susceptibility to the wind but tends to be less crowded due to the length of the paddle to get to it; The Bombie, a big chunk out back which can link through to The Peak with a high tide and big swell; The Peak, which breaks in front of the cave and gets very hollow and crowded but can link to Racetracks on a decent enough swell; Racetracks, the inside section offers dredging pits over a very shallow reef, and Outside Corner to the right of Racetracks, which only breaks when it is big, and can get beyond massive. Access is through the famous cave, and at high tide it can be quite sketchy getting in, and if you miss it you will end up at Padang.

AIDAN SALMON THREADS A HIGH SPEED PERISCOPES PIT.

PERISCOPES, SUMBAWA

Fun right hander with great shape that breaks a couple of clicks north of Lakey Peak on a long reef sticking out south of the headland. The paddle out is short but can be a headache as when it's big the current here is strong, taking you away from the action. You'll need a high line from take off to keep it in the sweet spot, but the hollow sections are fast with rampy shoulders and a clean exit into the channel. It is best at high tide when there is enough water over the reef, is offshore on a north wind and can hold up to about 8ft.

G-LAND, JAVA

The definition of left-hand perfection, G-Land is recognised the world over as one of the most magical waves ever found. After a long trip overland/ferry/overland through the east Javanese jungle you come to Grajagan Bay, home of the famous 2km-long point which holds consistent swell and rifles lines for hundreds of metres through several breaks which, albeit rarely, can link up to give you the ride of your life. Best on an east wind, the outer break at the top of the point is Kong's, which can hold the biggest swell and breaks with workable walls and the odd pitching section. Next up is the jacking Moneytrees, a long and demanding peak which holds large swell and fires mechanical barrels down the reef for a few hundred metres and can get sharp and shallow at low tide. Depending on the swell direction, you may need to take a high line to not get overtaken on this section, and it can sometimes link up with the inside reef. There is an additional takeoff area between peaks, Launching Pads, which sporadically breaks further out on big days and can join sections into the infamous Speedies. This is where you need to push hard, scoop, drop a cog and gun it for a couple of hundred metres as you will be locked inside the heaviest, fastest, roundest barrel at G-Land and it gets shallower the further it runs. If you have somehow timed your trip so the swell, wind, tide and lunar factors all conspire to link all the sections, you may well have just come off a wave you will never top.

IN MANY PEOPLE'S OPINION G-LAND IS THE BEST LEFT IN THE WORLD.

PIPING

ROB BARBER LAUNCHES A SKETCHY INVERT AT THE SPEEDIES SECTION AT G-LAND.

ALEX WILLIAMS

WITH THE EVER BUSIER LINEUPS IN INDONESIA, SEARCHING OFF-THE-RADAR ISLANDS CAN UNEARTH SOME TROPICAL PERFECTION.

KERAMAS, BALI

Located on Bali's east coast, right-hand Keramas picks up decent swell and breaks with good shape over a submerged lava reef close to shore. After a quick drop and scoop you stall to race the curtain and pop out to take on the end section before it shuts down in front of the volcanic black sand beach. Due to its location Keramas works best on a NW wind, and can provide good early-bird glass walls.

NATE LAWRENCE

"I love Keramas, I got so lucky there to score it pretty uncrowded, it's such a sick wave to surf , to draw a line and bust big, you can become a very capable bodyboarder surfing Keramas often, it helped me improve a lot going right." Pierre Louis Costes

CANGGU, BALI

Further up the coast from Seminyak on Bali's south west coast, Canggu is a skatepark for bodyboarding, loads of wedgy, barreling peaks. The reef bottom is partially covered by black sand which does shift around, so the peaks can periodically increase or decrease in quality. It is best to surf it early in the morning to avoid the crowds, which have risen in recent years and can be a problem. Luckily there are a few take off zones so the pack can spread out. It works throughout the tides although mid is often most consistent with good cover ups and lips to hit. Canggu is open to S/SW/W swells, and a NE wind is bang offshore.

AIDAN SALMON JAMS A REVERSE.

PADANG PADANG, BALI

The jewel in the sparkling crown of Bali's Bukit Peninsula, Padang's crystal-green barrels draw people from all over the world to try their hand at picking one off from the jostling pack in the lineup. It's a picture-perfect green room tube. At Padang you pull in and remain cylindrically slotted from take off to pull off. The wave breaks quickly and picking a speed line is important to make the end section which sucks faster as it runs out of water on the very sharp coral reef. Padang starts to turn on over 6ft, and is bizarrely safer at that size as there is more water covering the reef, which at 3ft is uncomfortably shallow but solely the domain of bodyboarders.

"WE LOVE YOU LONGTIME!"

MICKEY SMITH

ROB BARBER PULLS IN TO A
GREEN AFTERNOON BAZZA.

BOOGVIBE

There is a huge population of travelling bodyboarders and surfers in Indonesia. The allure of that perfect wave has long had riders the world over saving their pennies to book tickets to paradise. This of course has led to crowding problems on the more popular spots, but that is unfortunately the nature of the beast. Bali is the main destination, and although you can find a little basic sponge gear in shops here your best bet is to bring a couple of boards and spare kit with you. As it is pretty much the hub of the action you will no doubt meet many travelling bodyboarders here to hook up with and share boat costs if you want to escape the carnage and find your own slice of the Indo good stuff.

"Padang Padang Is one of those waves where the barrel is so intense and you think you won't make it, but I've had some bombs here, some of the deepest barrels I've had for sure."
- Pierre Louis Costes.

SUPER SUCK, SUMBAWA

A remote and fickle Sumbawan left located off Maluk Bay which takes a massive swell to break and is susceptible to local onshore switches even when the prevailing offshore trades are blowing. It is, however, one of the longest, meanest, inside-out left hand barrels you can get, honouring its name to the letter. Extremely shallow and sharp, it ledges heavily onto the coral shelf and churns its guts out at pace for a good length - previous barrel-riding experience is a necessity. Trusting your rail is as important here as anywhere in Indo.

SCORING SUPER SUCK IS SOMETHING THAT WILL
STAY IN THE MIND FOR EVER, ANDRE BOTHA
CLOCKING UP SOME SERIOUS TUBE TIME.

DESERT POINT ON LOMBOK, ARGUABLY INDO'S MOST PERFECT WAVE.

JASON REPOSAR

CHRIS BURT

LAKEY PEAK, SUMBAWA

One of the most fun spots in the world, Lakey Peak breaks both ways, giving a short hollow right (which can lengthen on the right swell direction) and a more popular left — a backdoorable A-frame which sets you up for an easy tube with all the trimmings. It can get very heavy on a low tide if there is enough swell, although both directions are best on mid. On bigger swell you start to see some serious bowls here, but unfortunately recent years have seen increasing theft on the beach, swollen crowds, and the vibe in the lineup is sometimes pretty tense. Get in early to make the most of the dawn glass before the onshores kick in.

INDO TRAVEL TIPS

The dry season is from May to September, when there is consistent swell and seemingly endless offshores. Indonesia is also ridiculously cheap, it is very easy to live on a minimum budget very comfortably for your whole stay. Food, accommodation and transport are all inexpensive, so depending on your budget you can kick back like a king on a fraction of the living costs of back home.

Kuta—Bali's party town— is a fun place to hang out, but be sure to escape before it sucks all your money away. Unless you step out of the craziness you won't experience the real Bali. It is distinctly different from the other islands, and is home to the vast majority of Indonesia's Hindu population. Bali's nightlife is the main drive of its economy, and since the awful terror attack in 2002 it has recovered well and quickly – there are now even more bars, clubs and ladyboys to tickle your fancy.

Indonesian transport is seemingly

RIGHT AND ABOVE; ALEX WAKE CLOCKING UP TUBE TIME GOING LEFT AND THEN GOING RIGHT AT LAKEY PEAK.

CHRIS BURT

WILL BAILEY

SANUR ON BALI.

JOHN CALLAHAN

ONE PALM POINT.
PACK A WETSUIT TO
PROTECT YOU FROM
THE SHALLOW REEF.

ONE PALM POINT, JAVA

A mystical wonder breaking off Panaitan Island, west of Java. This intense left-hand point barrels from take off all the way down the reef, and gets worryingly shallower the further you go. One Palm Point needs a quick drop, bottom turn and high line to make the barrel which stands up from the outset and keeps you kegged for as long as you dare. This is a heavy, serious wave a long way from anywhere which needs boat access from the westernmost tip of Java, several miles away. For all the risks though you are guaranteed empty perfection in a pristine jungle wilderness — what could be better.

devoid of rules, structure or safety, yet it somehow flows without too many problems. You can hire most forms of transport, and they're cheap with a capital C. If you are hoping to put in the hard yards to find new spots it might be worth splashing out on a 4x4, but the numerous little 110cc chicken-chasers are usually enough to burn you about from local spot to spot.

If you are expecting to be spending a bit of time on the road, expect the Balinese police to be on you like jungle mozzies. Carrying a full international driving license might help, but they have a reputation for hounding foreigners and never miss an opportunity to fine you for the smallest of things (even if they don't exist). Earmark some US dollars aside as your bribe fund. Your best bet is to try and avoid eye contact with them, their corruption is well known and even stories of drug dealers teaming up with police to plant, catch, and fine foreigners on the spot are not unheard of. Scammers and conmen are common, especially in the tourist trap Bali, so be vigilant. Only change your cash somewhere official, and don't get caught with drugs on you – this is a major deal here and can result in long prison sentences and even the death penalty.

Expect a fair amount of market hustle-and-pester whenever you are out and about in Bali – if you show the slightest crack of interest it's game over. You need to be friendly but firm with your 'no' to be left alone. Food is extremely varied and cheap, but despite your best attempts to monitor your diet the obligatory 'Bali Belly' is almost guaranteed. As with most developing countries, only drink bottled water and avoid ice cubes.

Don't wear green boardies when you are in Bali – myth has it that a local sea god doesn't like the colour green and most surfers who've met sticky ends have been donning the colour, so you've been warned!

PHIL HARNSBERGER TAKES TO THE KNEE AT PERFECT NIAS.

WILL BAILEY

"Bali offers the nights of your life, but for waves head out of Bali over to Sumatra or the outer islands to really get some perfection with half the people. If you're willing to really rough it you will find perfection to yourself." — Matt Lackey

LAGUNDRI BAY, NIAS

Not just the best right hander in Indonesia, but arguably the world. The point at Lagundri Bay gives you a picture-perfect almond-shaped green room, groomed with a gentle reverse-current which smooths out the walling faces which can comfortably reach 15ft. It has a good deal of power but peels at a precise pace without a drop out of place and eventually deposits you in a handy little rip which aids you nicely back to the peak — just in time for the next perfect set. After the 2005 Sumatran earthquake the reef was raised by a couple of feet, actually increasing the barrel length even further and allowing it to break from 2ft, whereas before it only started working properly over 4ft.

AUSTRALIA

THE HOME OF MODERN DAY BODYBOARDING

MITCHELL'S WEDGE, WESTERN AUSTRALIA.

> "For me, growing up in Australia on the Sunshine coast, the waves were small and fun, then I moved over to western Australia where some of the best waves in the world are. It changed my approach to how I want to ride waves, it definitely has waves that are comparable to Hawaii. I think Australia as a whole has some of the best, if not the best, waves in the world." - Jake Stone

WESTERN AUSTRALIA
LANGUAGE.....ENGLISH
MAIN AIRPORT.....PERTH INTERNATIONAL AIRPORT (PER)
CURRENCY.....AUSTRALIAN DOLLAR
SWELL SEASON.....YEAR ROUND, NORTH BEST MAY-AUG
WATER TEMP.....15C-22C SOUTH, 22C-28C NORTH

SOUTH AUSTRALIA
LANGUAGE.....ENGLISH
MAIN AIRPORTS..... ADELAIDE INTERNATIONAL AIRPORT (ADL), BRISBANE INTERNATIONAL AIRPORT (BNE)
CURRENCY.....AUSTRALIAN DOLLAR
SWELL SEASON.....YEAR ROUND, BEST MAY-OCT
WATER TEMP.....18C-24C

EASTERN AUSTRALIA
LANGUAGE.....ENGLISH
MAIN AIRPORTS..... SYDNEY KINGSFORD SMITH INTERNATIONAL AIRPORT (SYD) BRISBANE INTERNATIONAL AIRPORT (BNE)
CURRENCY.....AUSTRALIAN DOLLAR
SWELL SEASON.....YEAR ROUND, BEST DEC-MAR
WATER TEMP.....21C-26C

OUTLINE

The continent of Australia has 22,292 miles of coastline, which, as you might expect, yields a huge number of epic bodyboarding spots. Over the last two decades Australia has grown to become the centre of the global bodyboarding scene, boasting three world champions, numerous bodyboarding companies, IBA tour events and some of the heaviest waves ever tackled on a sponge.

To see the proper Australia you need to set aside a few months, buy a 4x4 and venture into the distance to seek and find. Despite many of the great waves being located relatively close to metropolitan areas, there are tens of thousands of insane waves off the beaten track. Just beware, that dusty track could be hundreds of kilometres long, and you can guarantee when you find the slab of your dreams, no one will be able to hear you scream.

BREAKS

With the exception of the Northern Territory and the landlocked Australian Capital Territory, every one of Australia's six states receives pumping swell and has incredible waves. From giant cold slabs in the south to tropical reefs breaking 50 miles offshore on the Great Barrier Reef, it ticks every box. Get a road map, fill a few jerry cans on the roof rack and enjoy the journey – it will guarantee you some crazy stories and absolutely sick waves.

SHARK ISLAND, NSW

The Island is one of the greatest bodyboarding waves on the planet, and is as heavy as 50 b*stards. After takeoff on the peak comes White Rock, a shallow ledge plastered with sharp barnacles which turns the wave inside out as it dredges further than you thought possible. Do not come off here, you will regret it instantly. The barrel at Shark Island is wider than it is tall, and the thickness of the lip comes second only to the mutant that is Chopes. That lip will blast all the water off the shelf and throw a shocky back into the barrel which you will battle to overcome before the wave turns to Surge. This end section is where it slows down, stands up and warps with boils before detonating onto a cunji-covered shelf with 3-4 inch barnacles ready to rip you to pieces. The wave breaks beyond shallow, sometimes dry, and is one of the most intense places you will ever take on. The crowd is often large and aggro, as the 'weekend warriors' from Sydney pop down to Cronulla on the train to get their fix. Works best on a SE/E swell with SW/W/NW winds. The Island is as intense a bodyboarding wave as anywhere in the world.

DAVE BALLARD NEGOTIATES HIS BOTTOM TURN ON A FLAT BOTTOMED BEAST.

TIM JONES

> "Shark Island has to be one of the most incredible waves that you can ride on a bodyboard. It breaks quite close to the land, is really shallow and the locals charge harder than anyone. Although a lot of people have been hurt there, it's a break that you just want to go to and score, it's so good." - Dave Winchester

LEE KELLY

The waters of Australia differ hugely in temperature; breaks off Tassie will require a 5/3mm wettie, whereas those in Queensland need nothing more than a pair of boardies and a thick layer of suncream. Expect to be able to get away with boardies as far south as Perth and Sydney in the summer, although you'll need to don at least a 3/2mm in the winter.

ACCOMMODATION

There are tens of thousands of backpacker accommodations around Australia, with a higher concentration on the more populated east coast. Most are cheap and cheerful, and located near some sick waves. The alternative is to get a camper and just park up close to wherever you want to surf. This is the ultimate deal in accommodation, doubles as your transport, and you can sell it after your journey. Get lucky and you may even be able to sell it for a profit, covering the cost of your trip.

BOOGVIBE

Bodyboarding has become a religion Down Under, with thousands of frothing groms charging the lineups of awesome waves around the country. In recent years the sport has taken off, in part due to footage of Aussie spongers tackling massive slabs which surfers wouldn't even be able to contemplate, and in general gaining a greater photo and media presence. This increased respect for the sport has spawned a bodyboarding micro economy. This growth has self-sustained the inception and development of Australian bodyboard, wetsuit and clothing companies, highly successful bodyboarding films, and the best magazines available. The Australian bodyboarding model is idolised the world over and is seen to be key in the growth of the sport, globally. As with anywhere, crowds are an issue on the more recognised spots, but there are literally tens of thousands of known and unknown spots in Oz which are totally sick, so get out your compass.

"Mechanical, it's almost feels like you're cheating at Blackrock because moves just feel that much easier to pull off. One of my favourite places in the world." - Dallas Singer

BLACKROCK, NSW

Otherwise known as Aussie Pipe, it is one of the best left hand reefs in Australia. Located on the SW side of the headland at the Jervis Bay Nature Reserve, it is way out in the sticks but is always crowded when it's on. A short, intense barrel over a sharp reef, Blackrock doesn't hold massive swell but has a sick boost section from the end bowl which wraps hard on the inside. Beware — some people here are not friendly, and cars frequently get broken into or damaged. Park unlocked with all your windows down, boot and glove box open to show you have nothing left in it worth stealing. You may still find broken windows. Walk through the brush from the car park til you find the cliff and carry round to the left, if it's working you will see the glory. The break works best on a SE swell with a NE wind.

LEE KELLY

WITH A PERFECT HIGH SPEED BARREL SECTION IN TO A PERFECT AIR BOWL, BLACK ROCK IS THE PLACE TO SEE WITNESS PERFORMANCE BODYBOARDING.

MITCHELL'S WEDGE, WA

Located south of Yallingup, this right hand wedge is heavy, hollow and powerful, offering deep scoops and big boost sections. It holds a large swell and gapes when the conditions line up. Sharks enjoy a good patrol of this coast south, so don't surf alone or at dawn or dusk to improve your chances, and that's if you find it — you are in the wild west out here. Works on a SW/W/ NW swell and is best on an east wind.

A MUTANT WEDGE THAT OFFERS SOME OF THE BIGGEST AND BEST LAUNCH RAMPS OF ANY WAVE IN OZ.

DURANBAH QLD

Commonly known as D'Bah, this very consistent beachbreak sits right on the border of NSW and QLD. Located just south of Snapper Rocks and the hellish backwash break of Froggies, D'Bah is a solid beachie with fast-breaking rights and lefts, which stand up hollow and throw out pits galore. Expect it to be rammed; this stretch of the coast is one of the busiest surf areas in the world. However, have patience and you will find some classic peaks which hold a good size. Works best on a SE/E/NE swell and W/SW wind.

UK DK MAESTRO ALEX MANNING SNAGS A WAVE FROM THE HUNGRY D-BAH PACK.

THE BOX, WA

Located just north of the famed Margaret River, this heaving right hand slab got its nickname from the shape it warps into as it barrels over a sharp shallow shelf a few hundred metres offshore. A short intense wave, it holds big swell and is quick to punish if anything less than 100% commitment is shown as you negotiate the steps and boils after your air drop. There is a reason the IBA hold the Australian leg of the world tour here. The Box works best on a big west swell and an E/SE wind.

MICKEY SMITH

TWO RIDERS DISPLAY THE BEST OF THE BOX;
BIG AIR TIME AND DEEP BARRELS.

MICKEY SMITH

AUSTRALIA TRAVEL TIPS

Australia is massive, but has a relatively small population, the majority of which lives in New South Wales and Victoria. Most people start their trips in NSW, as the cost of vans is usually cheaper, and you can get some crazily cheap deals as travellers start to freak out that they won't be able to sell their van before their onward flights. Check Gumtree.com.au for good deals in each city, or if you are in Sydney there is a weekly car gathering/auction near Kings Cross, where you can pick up a bargain. Expect it to have covered a million miles (on any number of previous engines) be covered with flowers and have beads hanging from the mirror. If you plan on leaving going off-road get a 4x4, and make it a Toyota. There is an expression in Oz – "If you want to go into the bush, take a Land Rover or a Land Cruiser. If you want to come back out, take a Land Cruiser." You will need to properly stock up on essentials if you plan a beast of a roadie, including loaded fuel and water tanks, spare tyres and a decent tool kit. The bush is not a place you want to be stuck in without supplies; some people have never been found.

Australia boasts all ten of the deadliest spiders in the world, numerous types of deadly snakes, scorpions, and that's before you get into the sea, which in southern areas (WA, South Australia, Tassie, Victoria and NSW) include great white sharks. The obvious advice with avoiding shark attacks is to not surf at dawn or dusk, aim to surf with other people, and not to tempt fate by paddling out where there have been known attacks.

If you are between 18-30 and want to work during your stay you can get a Working Holiday Visa, which allows you to travel and work in Australia for up to 24 months. If you don't plan on working you can get a tourist visa (ETA) which allows you up to a 3 month stay on each arrival up to 12 months from the date the visa was granted.

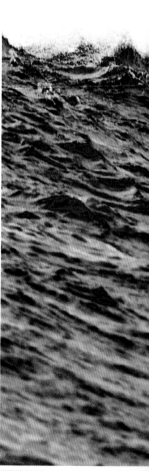

A BUSY DAY AT KIRRA.

WHEN THE SUPER BANK FROM SNAPPER TO KIRRA IS ON FORM, THERE ARE BARRELS AVAILABLE FOR UP TO 20 SECONDS. JACK JOHNS SNAGS A NICE TUBE AT KIRRA.

KIRRA, QUEENSLAND

Formerly Australia's longest barrel, the golden days of Kirra's famous 1km-long 30-second green room are sadly behind it due to excessive sand pumping into Coolangatta Bay. There is currently a campaign to get the sand pumped from Kirra to try and restore it, but as yet it remains stricken and closing out when it's small. However, despite it losing its consistency, on a big swell the Kirra of old lights up again, and it is a beautiful sight to behold; Large SE groundswell strikes and reels mechanically at 45 degrees down the point, throwing fast green tubes in a need-for-speed rush from as far back in the barrel as you dare to stall. Works best in a big SE swell and a west wind but beware of the ridiculous rip, it is probably better to get out and jog back up to the headland for your next pit than paddle against the current. Located just north of Snapper Rocks and Rainbow Bay.

THE HIGH RISES OF SURFERS PARADISE WATCH ON AS A PERFECT KIRRA PIT PEELS OFF.

SNAPPER ROCKS, QUEENSLAND

Located on the Gold Coast at the border of QLD and NSW, Snapper has become one of the most renowned right-hand point breaks in the world. Only a few of the many hardened locals take off at the peak behind the rock, but once it's thrown out and detonated the wave sucks hard into a thick pit which reels into the Superbank, where most of the waiting pack sit. Depending on swell direction and the state of the bank, this barrel dredges and sucks hard for an age before walling up into the next section, which can take you a couple of hundred yards. Near the peak it is brutally heavy and shallow, and the rip here is hideous. Many people attempt the all-or-nothing option of jumping out off the rocks between sets, as when it's big paddling out in Rainbow Bay will have you down at Kirra in no time. Works best on a SE/E swell — too much north in the swell direction and it will close out, too much south it will miss the best of the bank. Beware of crowds, when it's on it's a circus out there, but be patient and you will have the barrel of your life.

IF YOU CAN MANHANDLE A WAVE TO YOURSELF AT SNAPPER ROCKS YOU CAN RACE THE TUBE FOR OVER 100 METRES AT A TIME. THE RIP CURRENT IS FIERCE SO BE PREPARED TO PADDLE HARD TO STAY IN THE TAKEOFF ZONE.

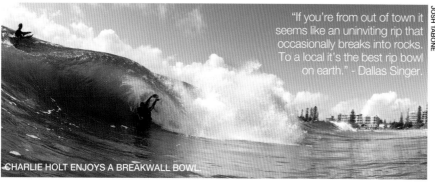

CHARLIE HOLT ENJOYS A BREAKWALL BOWL.

"If you're from out of town it seems like an uninviting rip that occasionally breaks into rocks. To a local it's the best rip bowl on earth." - Dallas Singer.

JOSH TABONE

BREAKWALL, NSW

A sick right hand wedge off the breakwall at Port Macquarie, over the river from the Town Beach Park. Super fun, hollow and breaking over sand, Breakwall offers up some wrapping barrels and very boostable bowls. It is home to some of the most talented up-and-coming bodyboarders in Australia, who all perfect their game here when it's on. The break refracts swell off the rock wall and opens up one of the best wedges on the east coast.

SMILLY

STRADBROKE ISLAND, QUEENSLAND

Considered by many as one of the best beachbreaks in Australia, South Stradbroke Island sits south-east of Brisbane but north of the craziness on the Goldy. Breaking hollow right and left over a shallow sandbar, Straddie is a powerful beachie that offers up short heavy barrels and boost sections. It works best on an E swell with W winds. Expect crowds and bowls galore.

"South Straddie is Australia's answer to Mexican Pipe. A-frames all over the place due to the outside bombie that breaks the swell up as it comes to shore. Heard a few guys call it the best beachbreak in Australia." Dallas Singer

CHRIS GURNEY

MANDURAH, A HIGH PERFORMANCE BODYBOARDING WAVE WITH SOME AWESOME TUBES AND RAMPS.

CHRIS GURNEY

MANDURAH WEDGE, WA

A predominant right hander with the odd left which wedges off a rock wall into a playground of bowls, boosts, backwash and big airs, breaking over sand. A dream wave for lovers of right hand wedge bowls. Usually packed with local rippers when it's on, expect a frosty reception if you paddle out with attitude — be patient and the odd peak will be sure to eventually wedge your way. Can handle some sizey swell and if timed right the air sections are utterly ridiculous. Works best on a W swell and E wind — get in early before the Fremantle Doctor blows it out.

PACIFIC ISLANDS

A BOUNDLESS BLUE FRONTIER OF FLAWLESS TROPICAL PERFECTION

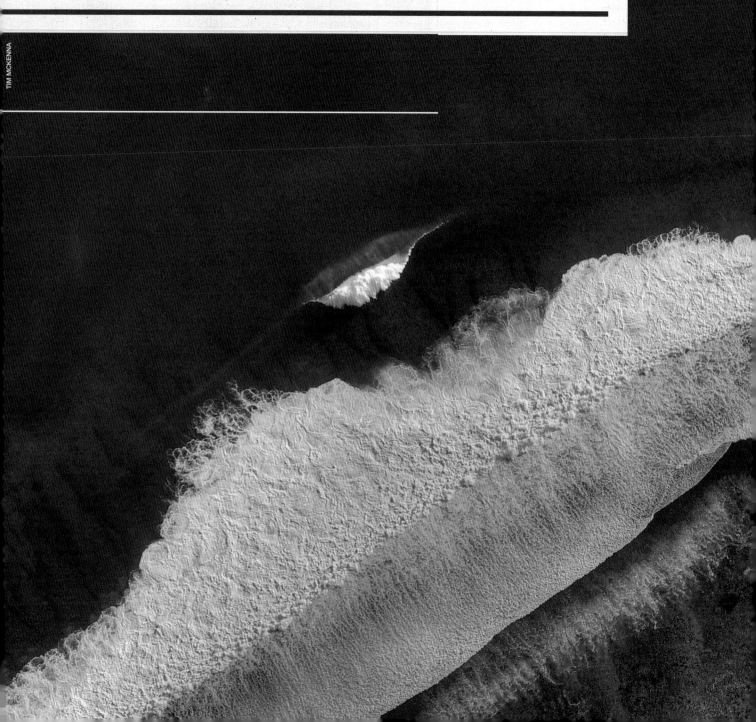

TIM MCKENNA

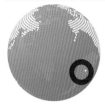

LANGUAGE.....**VARIOUS,**
TAHITI – FRENCH / TAHITIAN
MAIN AIRPORT.....**VARIOUS,**
TAHITI – FAA'A INTERNATIONAL AIRPORT (PPT)
CURRENCY.....**VARIOUS,**
TAHITI – FRENCH PACIFIC FRANC
SWELL SEASON.....**YEAR ROUND, BEST MAY-OCT**
WATER TEMP.....**25C-29C**

OUTLINE

Comprising of tens of thousands of islands disparately spread across the biggest ocean on earth, it is not surprising the Pacific Islands are home to some of the greatest waves ever found. Located beneath the tropic of Cancer, the island groups of Polynesia, Melanesia and Micronesia are a veritable playground of beautiful, tropical, reef-break barrels. Where the islands in Melanesia are often hilly or even mountainous, many of the tiny atolls and coral islands of Micronesia and Polynesia are low-lying with fringe reefs, which serve to protect the islets from big surf, and offering 360-degree reefs for multiple swell/wind combinations.

While breaks such as the fearsome Teahupo'o in Tahiti and perfect Cloudbreak in Fiji are world-renowned, the scope for new bodyboarding discoveries in the Pacific Islands is truly without boundary...the only limitation is how much money and time you have to spend. It boggles the mind to consider how many pristine reef passes are right now flawlessly breaking off uninhabited islands, just waiting to be discovered.

BREAKS

Due to the nature of how the atolls, islets and islands were formed, many of the best waves are found breaking off passes on the fringe reefs surrounding the islands. Where a shallow coral shelf meets a deep water channel you are likely to find a

TEAHUPOO, TAHITI

The most infamous wave in the world, Teahupoo, or Chopes, as it has become known, is one of the heaviest, gnarliest and scariest waves ever taken on. The sheer volume of water in each wave is almost unbelievable, as the entire Pacific trips over the shallow shelf off this little southern corner of Tahiti. As the swell builds and sucks water off the coral, a mountainous wall stands up square — seemingly defying physics — before unleashing a lip so thick it detonates the water in the flats out of existence in a ferocious explosion which booms down the reef ahead of a glassy face which has no back. When you pull in here you are actually below sea level...the back of the wave is the ocean itself. Some of the most spectacular waves, competitions, freesurfs, tow-surfs and wipeouts have happened here, and it has claimed lives in the blink of an eye. Teahupo'o wasn't even considered rideable until bodyboarding legends Mike Stewart and Ben Severson booged it in 1986. In 1998 the Gotcha Tahiti Pro competition brought it to the world's attention, and after Laird Hamilton's 'Millennium Wave' and the Tahiti Skins event in 2000 the place went off the dial. Simply put, Chopes is as heavy, intense and critical a wave as has ever been ridden — the ultimate wave of consequence.

"Teahupoo: Simply one of the heaviest waves in the world, amazing and scary all at once." - Jeff Hubbard.

CHOPES SMOKING. LITERALLY.

potential spot as the swell peels off the reef into the safety of the pass. The shape and depth of the reef directly equates to how the wave breaks over it on any given swell.

BOOGVIBE

Bodyboarding at places like Tahiti is rapidly increasing, and the standard of riding by locals is absolutely inspiring. The way they tackle their waves is what performance bodyboarding is all about – charging giant waves from deep in a critical barrel to tweaking huge aerials out of big bowls. However, despite this high level of riding in places such as Tahiti, bodyboarding is still in its infancy in some Pacific island groups and never even heard of in many of them, so the boogvibe is fresh – a clean slate to go and explore. As such, bodyboard shops are an extreme rarity and not bringing enough kit for trips to more distant islands can cost you – yes, fin tethers and leashes can be fashioned out of vines if you have to, but it's better to just bring spares!

BRENDEN NEWTON DROPS INTO A CHOPES KEG.

IT'S DIFFEICULT TO IMAGINE A MORE
BEAUTIFUL AND AWE INSPIRING SPOT
THAN TEAHUPOO.

THE CHANNEL AT CHOPES CAN GET
QUITE CONGESTED ON BIG SWELLS.

SAPINUS, TAHITI

A heavy, fast and powerful left reef which can break similar to Teahupo'o
without quite the same intensity. Gives a fun little peak with ramp
section when small, but on a medium to big swell delivers a fast take off
to set your line for a grinding pit or scoop into the end section which
opens up into a launching pad off its thick shoulder. Sapinus breaks
out in front of Punaaula on Tahiti's west coast, and works best on a W/
SW/S swell and east winds. It can hold very big here, and the current
increases with size so keep an eye on your position. It can also get
crowded due to its obvious location in front of the town, and the fact it
is so damn fun.

ROB BARBER HIDES FROM THE PNG HEAD HUNTERS.

PACIFIC ISLAND TRAVEL TIPS

The fact bodyboarding is still a relatively new sport means we are in the lucky position to control how it is viewed by the people of the islands we wish to seek out. It is an opportunity to lay down a positive pathway for future trips, by being respectful to the locals, the landowners and the tribal chiefs. If you open a polite and considerate dialogue, bring gifts, engage the local people with a smile (even if you have no idea of the language) and leave kit behind for their children to learn on, return trips will be welcomed.

The places which have been commercially developed (for surf camps, honeymoons or luxury holidays) can be quite expensive, but there are great swathes of Pacific Island groups where you can stay, travel and explore on a comparative shoestring. While some islands depend on tourism, some don't even know what it is. The beauty of travelling here is the isolation from the western world, meeting new people, immersing yourself in distant cultures and tracking down some undiscovered waves in paradise. All of the countries have rich and fascinating histories, traditions and cultures, so take some time on your trip to learn about the islands and you'll find your trip a lot more rewarding.

Most of the spots in the Pacific Islands will require hired boat trips or long paddles across lagoons to get to, so a decent pair of waterproof binoculars will help your search from the land no end. You soon learn what looks like an easy 15 minute paddle to the waves is in fact a grueling hour-long lagoon marathon which leaves you knackered by the time you get out there and needing to reserve enough energy (and daylight) after your session to make the paddle back. It's always best to ask around for fishermen who'll be willing to take you out to a few passes to find the best conditions and where you can jump in fresh and surf till sundown. At more popular or well-known surf destinations this could cost upwards of $50-$60 USD per half day (usually operated by the resort) but in the lesser-known areas some local fishermen are usually happy to take you out to

TWIGGY'S, PAPUA NEW GUINEA

Small wave heaven, Twiggy's is a beautiful draining little righthander near Manus Island which holds a perfect shape and zips along the coral ledge just begging to be booged. The sublimely tapering lip line makes playing in and around the tube feel like hide and seek. You can stall on takeoff, hang in the barrel, come out with a move then sit in the shade for a while longer. Lulls between sets can be a while though, and due to its equatorial location the tides can be somewhat erratic. About as fun a wave as you could ever have at 3ft, Twiggy's is proper surf frontier material, and one of numerous amazing little setups in the Admiralty Isles of PNG which remain largely unexplored.

reefs and sit around fishing or watching for hours for no more than a few bucks. If you do take the less beaten path it is good practice to tip a little – it leaves a good vibe.

Some islands are owned by tribal chiefs, who also own surrounding reefs. If you are looking to stay and surf a break for a few days it is advisable to ask for the village chief and bring a gift, he should take kindly to the respect shown and allow you access to the waves. Simply rocking up to pitch a tent is bad form and may see you in a spot of bother, so be humble. Even if you have a chartered boat, a gift for the chief may still be needed depending on which country you are visiting and where you have anchored it – your captain should know the score.

BARBER RACES YET ANOTHER PERFECT RIGHTHAND BARREL.

Going off the radar in PNG

By Rob Barber

Admiralty Isles in Papua New Guinea. It's the only place I've ever been on a surf trip and not seen hide nor hair of another waverider (apart from the local fishermen who catch the odd line of whitewater in their canoes).

When the weather was sunny the wind stayed light, unlike most other major surf destinations, probably due to the incredibly small land mass. It didn't go onshore as the day grew hotter, although there were often four or five totally different weather conditions in one day. Due to the position on the equator the tides were freakish as well, with a relatively small tidal movement but no real pattern to it. For example, high tide might be 2pm on a Wednesday but the next day it could be earlier by an hour or two or exactly the same time or an hour later. It was so weird not being able to get in to synch with it.

The gaps between the set waves in PNG were the longest that any of us had ever experienced. It was as if the place could do with a bit of a Viagra kick, with literally ten minutes or more between some waves. Like waiting for a bus, you'd sit on your board, basting in the equatorial sun and chatting, then there'd be a flurry of five or six waves and everyone would come to life, get shacked, then paddle back out and resume the banter. If you were out of position and missed a set it was heartbreak material. If you timed it right you could paddle back to the boat after your barrel, grab a drink and be back to the takeoff spot in time for the next set. The waves here are so fun and the sky at night was like nothing I've ever seen before — no light pollution for thousands of miles meant that the stars were absolutely awesome.

A little bit of reading about PNG had lead me to be slightly concerned about 'The Rascals' — a crazy marauding gang who rape and pillage the area around Port Moresby where we spent a couple of nights on our way to meet our boat. These guys operate above the law and as a result our hotel had a razor-wired wall and armed guards. I was also told about the man-eating saltwater crocodiles, and last but not least, the island locals who still have a penchant for cannibalism! As usual, the time spent worrying was totally wasted. The locals were so curious that they started to attempt to catch waves on their canoes, then after a few days moored at Twiggy's some local kids paddled out on a tree trunk to do some Polynesian-style wave sliding. They were so generally friendly, the absolute opposite to localism. I gave them one of my boards and a pair of fins when I left, so hopefully they'll be ripping by now.

Before I knew it, it was time to start my three days of travelling by boat and plane to get home. In our world of 'bigger is better', with gnarly waves being the current trend, we went off the radar a little and felt as though we'd experienced a perfect new small-wave frontier.

WITHIN AN HOUR OF ARRIVING AT THE FIRST REEF PASS, A SHARK HAD SWUM BENEATH OUR BOAT AND I'D SPOTTED A CROCODILE JAW HANGING FROM ONE OF THE PALM TREES ON A NEARBY ISLAND, A BIT LIKE A CRYPTIC WARNING FROM AN ANCIENT TRIBE. 100 percent isolation is the only way that you can describe time spent around the

SWILLY

RAY COLLINS

HUBB BOOSTS A MASSIVE TRADEMARK INVERT, CHECK
OUT THE DROP THAT HE'S GOT TO DEAL WITH!

YOU WOULD STRUGGLE TO FIND A HOLLOWER, MORE PERFECT RIGHTHAND BARREL IN THE WORLD. HUBB BOTTOM TURNS IN TO A DRAINER.

"P-Pass is one of the great right hand reefs, shallow running barrels with big air sections. It is so remote, tropical and beautiful." - Jeff Hubbard

P-PASS, CAROLINE ISLANDS

One of the most picture-perfect right hand tubes you could wish for, P-Pass breaks off of Pohnpei in the Caroline Islands in a whirl of technicolour blue and deep crisp barrels. It has been described as a miracle; a flawless, perfect sumptuous right hander which wraps off the reef into the Palikir Pass with transcendent superiority. Can be surfed on all tides but gets a tad shallow at low. East winds groom the swell which is best from the north, but can break from W to NE. You can only reach P-Pass by boat, so ask around on the island for one and you should be good, but you'll have to refer to it as Palikir Pass so they'll know where you mean. It is breaks like P-Pass that make the world a beautiful place.

FIJI

LET 'FIJI TIME' DICTATE YOUR QUEST FOR PERFECT BLUE BARRELS ... BULA!

LANGUAGE.....**ENGLISH / FIJIAN / HINDUSTANI**
MAIN AIRPORT.....**NADI INTERNATIONAL AIRPORT (NAN)**
CURRENCY.....**FIJIAN DOLLAR**
SWELL SEASON.....**YEAR ROUND, BEST APR-OCT**
WATER TEMP.....**25C-29C**

OUTLINE

Fiji is a diverse group of South Pacific Islands nestled halfway between New Caledonia and American Samoa. From the mountainous main islands of Viti Levu and Vanua Levu in the west and north, to the tiny sandy atolls of the Lau Group in the east, the tropical Melanesian group sits around 1,300 miles north east of New Zealand.

It has literally thousands of breaks to all swell directions, many undiscovered, and almost all coral reefs. The Mamanuca Islands in the south west hold some of the most perfect waves in the world, exposed to predominant SW groundswell from the Tasman. Can be prone to inconsistency with wind, but when it's on, there is nowhere better.

BREAKS

The Mamanucas are where the famed spots of Cloudbreak, Mini Cloudbreak, Wilkes Passage, Namotu, Swimming Pools and Restaurants can be found. In July 2010 the controversial surfing monopoly held on certain spots was lifted under the Regulation of Surfing Areas Decree, allowing anyone to surf these previously-private world class waves. The prevailing SE trade winds blow all year, but are usually stronger in the dry season of April to October. Spring and autumn are when the surf is best, and expect reeling lines into gorgeous crystal-clear caverns.

"Cloudbreak is the scariest place I have surfed in terms of long hold-downs. It's also one of the most amazing waves in the world in terms of big tubes." - Damian King

AN AWESOME LEFT HAND TUBE THAT HOLDS MAHOOSIVE SWELLS.

CLOUDBREAK

Up there as one of the best left handers ever found. Breaking five miles out from Viti Levu's Momi Bay, the wave can hold massive SW/W/NW swell. Long walls grind their way down the reef, peeling fast and hollow into powerful tubes. When big it links its main three sections into a very long ride, similar to G-Land. Best to surf at mid-high tide as at low it gets sketchy to the say the least. Now open to the public, there has never been a better time to sample one of the all-time greats.

ONE THAT GOT AWAY.

ROD OWEN

WHEN IT'S BIG YOU'VE GOT TO BE PREPARED TO PAY THE ULTIMATE
PRICE. KINGY GOT A TWO WAVE HOLD-DOWN DURING THIS SESSION
WHICH IS THE WORST HE'S HAD IN HIS WHOLE LIFE. PROBABLY ENOUGH
TO FINISH OFF A LESSER MORTAL!

SWIMMING POOLS

The right at Namotu Island, so called because of the clarity of the water. Not as long, big, or as intense as Wilkes Pass, it is usually smaller than its neighbour Namotu Lefts, but is faster and shallower.

RESTAURANTS

A more fickle but incredible left which is a rival for any wave in the world on its day. Best surfed at low as currents get stronger at mid/high. A mechanically tubular wave that rifles over a very sharp reef, expect to shed blood if you catch a rail here, the reef is unforgiving. Requires full commitment, and is offshore on the SE trade winds.

MINI CLOUDBREAK

More fickle than its bigger sister and renowned for being heavy and extremely shallow, don't even think about it at low tide, the reef will eat you. Works best on an E/N/NE wind and SW/W swell. Not quite as consistent as the more famous breaks further to the north, but a still world-class left on its day.

WILKES PASSAGE

A long and walling right, over the channel from Namotu Lefts. More exposed to swell, it has several peaks which work at different sizes. Best at mid-high tide, the reef can get a little too exposed at low. Wilkes works best on a SW swell/NE wind, and gets very heavy over 10ft. Drawing a clean line off the bottom turn to maximise trimming speed is important when there is more south in the swell as hollow sections can break quite quickly.

NAMOTU LEFTS

Another left hand reef breaking over coral, directly in front of Namotu Island. Slightly more sheltered than the more exposed Cloudbreak, Namotu Lefts is more mellow but still holds its own as one of the classic waves in the region. Works best on a SW swell/NE wind.

BOOGVIBE

There isn't a huge bodyboarding scene in Fiji but you may well meet fellow travelling barrel-hunting boogers. At almost all the spots stand-ups outnumber bodyboarders many times over, but as that puts you in the minority expect a bit more respect by locals for tackling the waves on a bodyboard – almost all the riders you share waves with will be zinc-clad surfers. As with many places in the world; smile, show respect and you will get it right back.

FIJI TRAVEL TIPS

Fiji is one of the most beautiful places you could ever visit and the waves are world class, but as many people are poor you may receive some unwanted attention by shopkeepers trying to get you to come into their stores. Be polite and gracious, the Fijian people are generally extremely friendly, very welcoming and happy to meet you.

Make sure you have decent travel insurance and six months left on your passport before it expires. Fijian tourist visas are not required for nationals from many countries, and you can stay for up to 90 days.

Try Kava, a traditional Pacific Island drink made from the root of the kava plant, it has sedative qualities, leaving a tingling, almost anaesthetic sensation in your mouth.

Oh, and don't forget 'Fiji Time' – this is the general reason things are late, so chill out, don't expect everything to be clockwork, and soak up the perfect waves and laid back vibe.

UNITED STATES

HIT THE COASTAL HIGHWAYS AND FIND YOUR OWN SLICE OF THE AMERICAN DREAM

WEST COAST
LANGUAGE.....**ENGLISH**
MAIN AIRPORT.....**LOS ANGELES INTERNATIONAL AIRPORT (LAX)**
CURRENCY.....**US DOLLAR**
SWELL SEASON.....**CENTRAL AND NORTH OCT-APR, SOUTH YEAR ROUND**
WATER TEMP.....**10C-22C**

EAST COAST
LANGUAGE.....**ENGLISH**
MAIN AIRPORT.....**JOHN F. KENNEDY INTERNATIONAL AIRPORT (JFK)**
CURRENCY.....**US DOLLAR**
SWELL SEASON.....**SEP-APR**
WATER TEMP.....**2C-21C**

OUTLINE

The mainland United States is flanked by the North Pacific to the west and North Atlantic to the east, and is bordered by Canada and Mexico. The US has an immensely varied geography, from scorching south western deserts and great open plains to frozen Arctic tundra and giant mountains ranges, it is also faced with a great many natural hazards including tsunamis, earthquakes, volcanoes, hurricanes, flooding, mudslides, wildfires and tornadoes. The US has many of the world's greatest cities and landmarks, and prides itself on the mantra 'big is beautiful' – be it in buildings, cars or food.

Despite having long coastlines bordering three bodies of water, the main surf areas are located in Southern California and sporadic pockets on the east coast, with some cracking waves found on New York's Long Island. There is a great potential for spots in the Pacific Northwest and New England coasts, but with cold water and wild swells the majority of the surfing populace sticks to the more renowned yet crowded breaks of SoCal and the East Coast hotspots.

BREAKS

California can be divided into three areas; Northern, Central and Southern. Although the whole of the state's beautiful coastline receives surf, it's in the south where some of the better sponge waves exist, backed by consistent swell, great

> " T-Street has fun left and right beach break waves, great for practicing moves.." - Jacob Romero.

A GOLDEN VIEW FROM A MORNING CALI BEACHBREAK SESSION.

DAVID PUU

T-STREET, CALIFORNIA

The most popular break in the San Clemente area (other than the uber-crowded Trestles), T-Street is very consistent although the wave quality differs depending heavily on the swell direction, size and tide at any given moment. It generally works best at mid-to-high tides, although the Beach House peak works better on low. There are three main spots; Main Peak, Cropley's, and Beach House. Main Peak works best on large, long-period swells from any direction, but is best on a large northwest swell in winter with long, peeling pointbreak-style waves; Cropley's works best on a short period northwest wind swell combined with some southwest ground swell; and Beach House, which delivers some wedgy lefthanders on a straight south swell at low tide offering boostable little bowls for flips, rolls and variations. Oh, and T-Street is blackballed for standups in the summer daytimes making it a boog-only show, brilliant.

COULD AN IMAGE SOME UP CALIFORNIA MORE PERFECTLY?
IT'S EVEN GOT THE FATHER AND AND ADOPTED MOTHER
OF THE SPORT IN THE US — JAY AND VICKI REALE IN THE
FOREGROUND, ABOUT TO GO FOR A SURF.

NEWPORT WEDGE, CALIFORNIA

One of the most deranged waves ever tackled, Newport Wedge is a mutant shorey machine which greets massive south swells and wedges them up further into towering peaks, defying gravity just long enough to allow unhinged soldiers to drop in and ride her till she bucks…and buck she will, in spectacular fashion, resulting in some of the highest, heaviest, funniest and brutally dangerous wipeouts you will ever witness. It tends to work mostly in the summer months, and when it does, big crowds gather on the beach to witness the carnage. If you have some kind of gladiator/exhibitionist tendencies and you think you can handle it, this place is for you. Waves refract off the rivermouth groyne rocks south of the action, creating gnarly left hand side-wave shutdowns which kiss incoming shorey bombs in a cataclysmic explosion of water and sanity. Offshore on a N or NW wind, best at mid tide.

JEFF FLINDT

ONE OF THE HARDCORE LOCALS NEGOTIATES THE ELEVATOR DROP.

A CRYSTAL CALI BEACHBREAK PITCHES OUT, THIS IS A MUST-DO TRIP. JUST CRUISE THE PACIFIC COAST HIGHWAY, PICK A SPOT, GO SHRED THEN GRAB YOURSELF ONE OF THE WORLDS BEST BURGERS!

"Newport Wedge is easily the heaviest wave in Southern California with hard sand and thick lips." - Jeff Hubbard.

weather. While the wild north is savaged by giant cold Aleutian-born N/NW swells, the rugged and multi-directional central region is open to varying swell direction and a greater number of spots, although some can be very fickle. The south is the centre of the Californian bodyboard industry, and where many of the best spots break year-round and are seasonally groomed offshore thanks to the desert Santa Ana winds (October to February).

On the east side, New York's Long Island consists of 118 miles of SSE-facing coast almost perpendicular to the rest of the region's shoreline. It hoovers up southern groundswell into a succession of hollow beachies (and stone reefs off Montauk and the eastern tip) and is battered by hurricane and 'noreaster' winter swells which blast up the east coast.

BOOGVIBE

Bodyboarding in some parts of California is a lesson in self-defence, it's safe to say many of the older surfers don't take kindly to your chosen wave-riding tool and localism in a few popular areas is hardcore and regimented, but generally it's a free-for-all at most spots. Crowds are a constant problem in Southern Cali, but it's to be expected when you consider the sheer numbers of waveriders living close to the beach. While the spots mentioned in this guide are some of the best on their day, there are decent sponge setups littering the coast from Ventura down to the Mexican Border; including Seal Beach, 40th Street in Newport, Aliso and several hidden coves in Laguna Beach, Lower Trestles, Oceanside Pier, Seaside Reef and it's inside shorebreak section 'Parking Lot's', Black's Beach and the adjacent reefs, and Imperial Beach to name but a few. Bodyboarding is booming in California, and backed by a strong industry, is just what the sport needs.

New York and Jersey are often overlooked but have hardened families of bodyboarders who pride themselves on their dedication in surfing cold and wild waves throughout winter, at temperatures Southern Californians wouldn't contemplate. These tight crews of boogers rip, and don't shirk the eye-watering concept of crossing New York City in a car at rush hour just to check out a few ice-cold dark peaks if there is a sniff of NW on the wind and a bump in the North Atlantic.

JEFF FLINDT

GETTING BARRELLED IN THE OC! A WORLD AWAY FROM THE
PLASTIC SURGERY, DESIGNER DOGS AND BLOWN UP BOOBS
THAT ARE RAMPANT ON THE TV PORTRAYAL OF THE AREA.

SALT CREEK, CALIFORNIA

A crowded playground of decent breaks located in Orange County,
halfway between Huntington Beach and Oceanside. Salt Creek is
broken down into The Point, a lefthander with small takeoff zone
which picks up solid south swells and lays them down nicely into
chargeable walls across the bay; Middles, where the majority
of the pack sits and where punchy, fast and occasionally hollow
right and lefts break over a sand bottom; and Gravels, the best
boog spot, throwing up slabbing shorebreak-esque barrels breaking
over a shallow abrasive sandbank. Gravels does have a tendency to
close out, but with a solid combo swell from both the south and
northwest (which is common in autumn and spring) you are almost
guaranteed a deep, makeable barrel. Any wind from a south through
northeast direction will mean clean conditions, and it's one of the
few sheltered spots on 'south wind' days. It also offers a thick
kelp bed outside the break that keeps surface conditions smooth
long after most other adjacent spots have blown out. All spots get
hideously crowded when they're on, but get out on the dawny for your
share of the waves.

US TRAVEL TIPS

In the US the car is king, and although there are good public
transport links in and around metropolitan areas, you are best
off renting a car to get from spot to spot. If the SoCal crowds
are too much, Central and Northern California offers a wild and
challenging alternative, so much so you wouldn't think you were
even in the same state. Fog-shrouded headlands forested with
giant redwoods rise far up behind the cold and swell-lashed
beaches, although finding a quiet, sheltered cove which might
benefit from the prevailing northwesterlies is harder than you
think. Likewise on the east coast New England is home to some
epic coldwater points and flatstone reef setups, miles away from
New York and New Jersey's barrelling shories. The further you
work your way north on either coast the more you escape the
crowds and start to appreciate modern wetsuit technology.

Fortunately fuel is cheap in the US compared to some
European countries, and there are a multitude of cheap motels
and motor lodges for roadtripping adventurers looking to find a
booming East Coast barrel or rolling Golden State A-frame.

Watch out for water quality in the LA area; while there are
some good spots, the health risk involved with duckdiving
through some of the foulest, filthiest and most hideous city
run-off is a genuine worry. It's not just the general street filth of
bacteria and chemicals, but the used syringes and excrement
that is washed out of LA in heavy rains straight into the lineups.

As for the East Coast, forget Long Beach in the summer
– it is a zoo of New Yorkers escaping the sweltering heat of
the city to splash around off Long Island to cool down. Add
this to frequent long flat spells and militant lifeguards and you
have a reason to come back in the more quiet autumn, when
the southern hurricane swells march up the coast and pack
the beaches with punch after punch. If you have a decent
wettie and gloves, winter is a consistent period for the upper
east coast, but wading through snow to get into the icy water
requires a certain mindset.

It is not just New England, New York and New Jersey
which have good surf — much of the East Coast has spots,
although many in the Carolinas and Georgia break on the
offshore barrier islands. While North Carolina's Outer Banks
hold some solid and empty barrels, South Carolina and Georgia
suffer with a continental shelf which drains all
but the biggest swells of much of their power.
The man-made groynes here offer up some
respite in the form of the odd hollow peak over
forming sandbars, but there is still a fair bit
of exploration to be done on these southern
outer banks — and with it some fun potential
for the boog.

Further south, Florida isn't what would
be considered a bodyboarding hotspot,
although there are a few breaks which fire up
on long-period hurricane swells and the more
reliable noreaster swells that rake through
from October to April. Breaks like Wabasso
(near Vero Beach), Jupiter Inlet, New Smyrna, Sebastian Inlet,
Reef Road and Pump House can all hold decent waves on
their (albeit rare) day, and if you're looking to escape the chilly
northern climes for a cheap tropical vacation, Florida offers
plenty of touristy diversions with comfortable temperatures,
and warmer water.

"Lido Beach: a super fun beach
break with cute peaks great
for bodyboarding, plus it's
conveniently close to the city."
- Jeff Hubbard

LUCIA GRIGGI

LIDO BEACH, NEW YORK

Lido is one of the best bodyboarding waves on Long Island. Sandwiched between the punchy peaks of Long Beach and Point Lookout, the whole stretch out to the Hamptons and beyond can turn on given the right conditions. The beachie at Lido can handle decent sized hurricane swell, and is best at low when it delivers powerful and hollow top-to-bottom tubes breaking over the sandbank. On a north wind they are held up nicely for a drop, scoop and barrel, and can run into fast boostable lips and sections going either way. It can get crowded, but there are many other spots to surf along the LI coastline, which on the whole works best on N/NW winds and S/SE groundswell.

JIMMY JOHNSON

JEFF HUBBARD RATES JENKS AS ONE OF THE PUNCHIEST EAST COAST BEACHBREAKS. MIKE MURPHY FLYING.

JENKS, NEW JERSEY

One of the best wedges on the Jersey Shore and beyond, Jenks breaks as a predominant left off the south side of the Manasquan Inlet at Point Pleasant. On a chunky swell Jenks will dish out some proper bowls over a sandbar bottom with ledgy peaks and hollow sections. Expect there to be a heavy crew on it with west winds. Jenks can hold solid swell from the south right round to the north east, it certainly ranks as one of the best boog spots in the region, and plays host to the annual USBA comp each year, a favourite on the tour.

PIPELINE,
OAHU

Perfect, huge, heavy, beautiful, hollow, critical,
mental and crowded are all suitable adjectives for
Pipeline, the most renowned and photographed wave
on the planet. A flawless creature from the shore,
surfing Pipe is a different ball game; expect
ridiculous crowds, sneaker sets, backwash, close-outs,
hold-downs, big rips, double-ups, fist fights, heavy
sections and snapped leashes. The winter months see
Pipe turn on with big W/NW/N swells refracting off
the outer reefs to unload with ferocious power on the
inside reef, which is shallow, sharp and riddled with
caves to trap you in. Watch out for swinging swell
with more east in it — it will turn a makeable line
into a punishing closeout in the time it takes you to
bottom turn and realise it's all gone wrong. When it
gets big, second and third reef Pipe starts to wake up
and yawn — don't get caught inside. Pipe works best on
a SE wind. When it's on there is nowhere else to be,
but with it must come patience (hours of it), fitness,
respect, and balls of solid rock.

HAWAII

LANGUAGE.....**HAWAIIAN / ENGLISH**
MAIN AIRPORT.....**HONOLULU INTERNATIONAL AIRPORT (HNL)**
CURRENCY.....**US DOLLAR**
SWELL SEASON.....**YEAR ROUND, BEST NOV-MAR**
WATER TEMP.....**25C-28C**

OUTLINE

The Hawaiian Islands sit slap bang in the middle of the biggest ocean on the planet, and as such get a huge amount of swell. The volcanic island group is the 50th US state and has a large variety of different breaks, from beaches and points to shories and reefs. Make no mistake, Hawaii is heavy — in its surf, its crowds, its tempers and its prices. The reward? Proving yourself in front of 10,000 photographers and the world's waiting media.

Hawaii has long been the hub of the bodyboarding world, with its centre the famous North Shore of Oahu. It is the annual testing ground for boogers the world over, and where the sport's best come winter after winter to hone their talent and nerve in some of the biggest and heaviest waves on the planet. Modern day bodyboarding owes its existence to the spongers who conquered the North Shore. Although there are superb waves up and down the island chain, Oahu is the main focus of the surfing world.

BREAKS

The 'Seven Mile Miracle' of the North Shore of Oahu faces NW and stretches between Haleiwa and Velzyland. It incorporates some of the best, most respected and heaviest waves ever surfed on a bodyboard. From the infamous Waimea Shorey through Log Cabins, Off The Wall and on to Backdoor and Pipeline, the stretch gives bodyboarders all they could wish for over the booming winter months of solid W to N swell. Summer months (May to September) bring south swells, which light up Makapuu and the boog-friendly Sandy Beach, on the south east corner of the island.

THE MAN AND THE WAVE THAT INSPIRED MILLIONS OF BODYBOARDERS. MIKE STEWART LOCKED IN BACK IN HIS '90S HEYDAY.

JUST WATCHING PIPE CRANKING FROM THE SAFETY OF THE BEACH IS AN EXPERIENCE IN ITSELF.

TIM JONES

"Off the Wall? It would have to be one of the most glorified closeouts in the world!" - Dave Hubbard

JACK JOHNS LAUNCHES OFF A NICE BOWLY CLOSEOUT!

OFF-THE-WALL, OAHU

Separated from Backdoor by a channel, OTW needs more north in the swell to make the rights makeable. Expect big crowds as ever, OTW is shallow, hollow and heavy, with a shorter lesser-quality left. Works best at mid tide on a N/NE swell on an easterly wind, it is a booger's dream and very consistent.

"Early season or late season are the best times to get waves. Even then, any tourist will find themselves at the bottom of the food chain out there." - Mark McCarthy

BACKDOOR, OAHU

The right hander at Pipe comes alive when the swell veers more round to the north, or north east. It is heavy, shallow, rippy, fast and more than likely to close out - expect air drops on takeoff and an ever-funneling blue barrel that locks you in and swallows you up. The vibe at Backdoor is just as heavy as Pipe, and can even be worse on big days as there is no channel. Backdoor is deceptive and brutal, and it works best on a SE wind.

BACKDOOR LOOKING FUN.

WAIMEA SHOREY, OAHU

Waimea Shorey wasn't even thought of as a rideable wave until bodyboarders gave it a stab, with spectacular consequences. Further into the bay from the famous Waimea big-wave spot, huge swells roll, snarl and warp into the bay breaking at up to quadruple-overhead and unloading in a diabolical mess of suicidal closeout shorey. If you want the flogging of your life, get involved, leash optional. Works best(?!) on a big W to NE swell and easterly wind, although, if you do attempt the shorey, the last thing on your mind as you push over the edge is whether the wind has too much south in it.

SHARPY

"For a bodyboarder travelling to Hawaii, first and foremost thing that you should do is cultivate a mindset of respect for the waves and for the local people. You get different types of waves all year round in Hawaii, but the waves in the winter on the north shore, especially at Pipeline, are a very unique surfing environment that every bodyboarder should probably experience."
- Mike Stewart

Oahu is not all about the North Shore, indeed some days there will be no point in paddling out – be it through 300 people in the water or 30ft hellsets. There are breaks all around the island, so be prepared to have a search and you may well strike gold – always be humble and share the stoke, not all locals are heavy, and you never know, if you find yourself in the right spot they may even hoot you in to a couple.

The Island chain of Hawaii is littered with waves outside of Oahu – if you have a little more money and enough time, get out to explore some of the other islands. Gems are waiting out there, and you are almost guaranteed fewer crowds.

BOOGVIBE

The bodyboarding scene in Hawaii is huge. From sponge shops to the lineups, you'll see bodyboarders everywhere flying the flag — tucking into turquoise shorey shutdowns or scooping into massive outer reef bombs. The influx of pros when the season kicks off is always a spectacle, and the

ANDREW RAMS

SANDY BEACH, OAHU

According to Jeff Hubbard the "day-to-day Mecca of bodyboarding in Hawaii", Sandy Beach features the beachie rights and lefts of Gas Chambers, Middles, Cobbles and Pipe Littles. Despite its name, Sandy Beach also has a fair share of rocks, and works best on an E-SW swell and NW wind. Has an extremely fun/heavy shorey, where, as you expect, boogers dominate. Can get hectic inside with crowds though.

PIPELINE OVERVIEW.

LOG CABINS

Just up the coast from Waimea Bay at Pupukea Beach Park sits Log Cabins, a shifty right hand reef which breaks over a sharp and nasty fingered reef which gets a little sketchy on bigger swells. Needs a fair bit of north in the swell direction to prevent horrible closeouts, but chucks a heavy barrel and works best on a mid to high tide with an easterly wind.

DAMIAN PRISK JAMS A REVERSE AT LOGS.

SACHA SPECKER

THE NORTH SHORE VIEW WE ALL CRAVE.

IBA/CATALANO

TUNGSTEN

TUNGSTEN

> "Pipeline is the main surfing stage of the world, if you are killing it out at Pipe, then you're a world class rider. It also has a lot of different faces; from fun to intense, to fearing for your life. The atmosphere out at big Pipe makes you appreciate being alive and relaxed on the beach."
> - Damian King

fact Pipe breaks just 30 yards off the beach means you can watch the best riders in the world putting on a show right in front of you.

Locals at the famed spots take priority, followed by the pros – after this the scraps are handed out to the masses. Tensions can rise when conditions turn on, so don't be cocky. Despite its heaviness, the bodyboarding vibe in Hawaii is good, and if respect is shown you shouldn't get burned. The general rule of thumb is to never drop in, be patient and let your bodyboarding do the talking.

TEMPS
The water is warm and boardshorts-friendly. Northeasterly trade winds cool the coast down and blow offshore on the

North Shore breaks, but Hawaii averages seasonal air temperatures of 27°C to 31°C 80°F to 90°F). Generally the climate falls into the dry season (May to October) and the wet season (November to April).

ACCOMMODATION
There are lots of accommodations on Oahu from luxury five star resorts to cheap hostels, but for lodgings close to the North Shore expect to pay more – especially when in peak season. Alternatively, locals will often offer rooms or sometimes whole houses for rent, which might work well if you have a group of friends to split the bill. Check the notice board at Foodland for vacancies.

Hawaii Backpackers has a variety of different living accommodations located near to Sharks Cove on the North Shore. The Main House is located across the street from The Pupukea Beach Marine Sanctuary and has spacious living areas, a fully stocked kitchen and cable TV.

HAWAII TRAVEL TIPS

Despite its reputation as a wave-drenched surfing paradise, the North Shore does have its flat spells and rainy onshore days. There's not a lot to do at these times, so this is when the seductive attractions of the city of Honolulu tempt you, be it a relatively innocent day at the mall, or a couple of hours stuffing dollar notes in a girl's garter at a strip club. A cheap bus service runs round the island if you don't have a hire car. Other things to do for flat day fun include hiking the hills above Waimea, or... well, that's about it really. It has to be said extended flat spells do send you crazy, as most boogers are here for one reason.

Be prepared when bodyboarding in Hawaii – there are fewer places more heavy and dangerous, the swell can quickly jump from 2ft to 12ft, and sneaker sets are common. It is not a place for the faint-hearted, but the rewards are huge, in every sense of the word.

Under the Visa Waiver Program, tourists are allowed up to 90 days in the US without a visa.

> "Kahului Harbour is one of the best spots on Maui. Real shallow and hollow. Doubles, triples, or even quadruples up on a super shallow reef." - Jacob Romero

DAVID BAKER

KAHULUI HARBOUR, MAUI

One of the sickest sponge spots on Maui, it gives insanely thick, ledgy, double and triple-up rights which break, reform and bowl onto the reef with a heavy, sucky barrel and square boost section. Needs a big NE swell to get going but is absolutely made for bodyboarding when it's on. Beware of crowds, kamikaze air-drop ins, and polluted water (due to its close proximity to a commercial harbour).

CHURCHES, MAUI

Kahului Bay on Maui's north coast is home to a couple of gems, one of them Churches; a fun little rivermouth spot which works best on a NE swell and SW wind to groom the offshores. The predominant rights give rampy shoulders and sections for fun punts. Located north of the harbour, take Ukali Road off Waiehu Beach Road (340) and the break is in front of Kanai Place on the left at the end of the road.

DAVID BAKER

CHURCHES SERVING UP SOME TASTY BOWLS FOR ITS SPONGE DISCIPLES.

HONOLUA BAY, MAUI

One of the finest waves on the island, Honolua Bay is an epic right hand point on the north west coast which peels fast, hollow and long. Best from the NW with a SE wind, it can hold massive swell which links several different sections giving long tubular walls, wide carveable shoulders and heavy boost sections. Beware of the rocks on the inside, and the heavy crowds when the corduroy comes.

CHILE
AN ARID COASTAL FRONTIER OF ENDLESS COLD WATER SLABS

LANGUAGE.....**SPANISH**
MAIN AIRPORT.....**COMODORO ARTURO MERINO BENITEZ INTERNATIONAL AIRPORT (SCL)**
CURRENCY.....**CHILEAN PESO**
SWELL SEASON.....**YEAR ROUND**
WATER TEMP.....**13C-20C**

OUTLINE

Although averaging just 109 miles wide, Chile has a coastline more than 4,000 miles long, tightly sandwiched between the South Pacific Ocean to the west and geologically active Andes mountains just to the east. Chile has more than three dozen active volcanoes in this range, the longest continual mountain range on the planet. Chile's unique position on the west-facing spine of South America sees an arid north (home to the Atacama Desert, the world's driest), Mediterranean middle and damp and cool south.

Just 100 miles off the Chilean coast lies the deep water Atacama Trench, the point where the Nazca Plate is being subducted beneath the South American Plate. This tectonic activity has seen many large earthquakes and tsunamis hit Chile, including the most powerful earthquake ever recorded on Earth in 1960, and 15 separate quakes of magnitude of 6.2 or greater in the last 30 years.

PETE GLEESON

BREAKS

With such a long coastline exposed to the Roaring Forties, Chile's endless kiss with the Pacific boasts many epic waves, featuring long points, heavy reefs and raw slabs. Chilean surf is extremely consistent and very powerful, due to open-ocean swells and the lack of a continental shelf to drain them of their energy before touching down. The oceanic Humboldt Current cools Chile's seawater from the south year round, but also its marine air, which results in lingering fog and clouds. The current is also responsible for the prevailing S and SE winds, which are best to take advantage of in the mornings to plunder the dark green glass. The north around Iquique and Arica is just made for bodyboarding with slab after slab, many of which are genuinely world class. The south is more of a frontier of points, but there is an awful lot of coastline in between which is inaccessible… the mind melts at the secrets it hides.

PETE GLEESON

WITH A BACKDROP OF THE ATACAMA DESERT, ONE OF THE MOST ARID REGIONS OF THE WORLD, INTENDENCIA ISN'T LACKING IN DRAMA.

HEAVY LIPS AND URCHIN RIDDLED ROCKS COMBINE TO MAKE INTENDENCIA A HARDCORE WAVE.

INTENDENCIA

Iquique's miniature Teahupo'o packs a heavyweight punch. Intendencia is a fast, thick, hollow, lefthand slab which needs 100 per cent commitment from the go to avoid being hung up in the lip and delivered a hideous slam into the flats. If you negotiate the scorpion drop expect a deep, intense barrel and a spit to freedom. Intendencia is super heavy and almost impossible to escape once you've committed. Needs a W/SW swell and N/NE wind to clean it up and increase the makeability of the heavy drops.

EL GRINGO

Chile's most famous bodyboarding wave is just seven miles from the Peruvian border in the far north of the country, breaking off the exposed Alacran Island at the town of Arica. A hollow and fast A-frame reef which throws critical kegs, the left is an intense scoop with gaping bowl to blast off, and can get very shallow inside. The right is a little longer but doesn't wrap as roundly as the left, which in addition to its air section can funnel fast barrels to the point of no return. A relatively short wave, El Gringo gets fearsome and can handle serious swell. It is best to surf in the mornings when the winds are more favourable, and on a high tide. NE winds are offshore, and it will pick up any swell from the south right round to the north west. Entry and exit is over the rocks, try to use the keyhole and it's a short paddle to the peak on all but the big stuff. Get it early morning and you should have it all to yourself for a while before the locals rise too.

PLC LAUNCHES A FLAWLESS AIR REVERSE OUT OF THE EL GRINGO BOWL.

BOOGVIBE

Chile is just made for high performance bodyboarding; how many insane reef setups and dredging slabs there are is anyone's guess, but of those that have been discovered many are absolutely world class. The consistency and power of the breaks makes for wave-rich trips, and although some of the more renowned spots can get crowded with the local crews, there are many empty breaks waiting to be conquered. The locals can get feisty in (and out of) the water, but if you arrive flying solo without an accompanying rent-a-crowd you will find them a good bunch of guys who are welcoming and happy to meet you. The level of riding on the better spots is – as you would expect — of a very high standard, and the dedication to charge Chilean hard is instilled from an early age.

CHILE TRAVEL TIPS

Large parts of the Chilean coastline are virtually empty, so do your research before you leave and study maps and nautical charts in the quest for setups. It is also worth talking to people who have previously visited Chile for advice, and who may even have a contact or two on the ground who'll have the heads up on local info during your stay.

It's a sad fact of life that police in developing countries are generally underpaid and use 'fines' to supplement their income, and despite being a middle power, Chile is no exception. They may try and pick you up for a minor (or even invented) offence, but it's best not to argue with them or get stroppy. Hand over the small fine (usually less than $20 US) and go on your way.

As a westerner in a developing country you may have more money in your pocket than some people earn in a year. As a result it's no real surprise that the locals will want to prize it away from you — usually legally (in their enthusiasm to sell you stuff) but sometimes illegally. Be aware, keep an eye on your gear and bring locks for your bags. Gringos have been known to be held up at gunpoint (even by kids) and attacked

HIT THE ROAD IN CHILE, THERE ARE STACKS OF AMAZING WAVES, IT'S NOT ALL ABOUT EL GRINGO!

for their cameras or the change in their pockets. Keep low key and try to avoid late night urban exploration around the dodgier districts.

Despite this, the nightlife in Chile is awesome and quite unique – many clubs are rammed with beautiful girls who all seem to find white foreign skin an attractive attribute, so congratulations. It starts after midnight in most places and some clubs (you'll have to ask around) have 'special' nights where live sex on stage appears actively encouraged for all in attendance. Leave your morals at the door.

Make sure to try local cuisines wherever you go — a good way to do it is to order the Menu del Dia (menu of the day) which is a two or three-course selection of local delicacies, which are super cheap, tasty and eye-opening.

The Chileans also love football, so get stuck in and you'll be sure to meet the local guys, some may even give you the key to a few locals secrets. Appear in the lineup a few times by yourself, show respect and you'll make friends and get your share of barrels.

"El Gringo is an unbelievable wave with one of the best left ramps I've ever had to pleasure of hitting. Everything after that part of the wave is scary." - Dallas Singer

EL RANCIO: PERFECTION IF YOU CAN SNAG A WAVE FROM THE FROTHING PACK.

EL RANCIO

A couple of miles south of El Gringo sits one of the best bodyboarding waves in the country. The name means "rancid" in English, thanks to the nasty fish factory effluent which makes the place (and you, post surf) stink. El Rancio is a right hand bodyboarding dream slab with a barrel from the off and all the way down the line into a massive boost shoulder — everything you could want from a wave. However, it does have a small takeoff zone and is always packed with the local spongers (no surfers!), so be respectful, learn some Spanish and share the stoke. El Rancio keeps its sick square shape even when small and works best on ESE winds and a W/SW swell.

Seek and ye shall find...

By Ryan Hardy

KINGY HAD BEEN PLANNING TO MAKE A CHALLENGING JOURNEY FOR ALMOST A YEAR AND AFTER A FAIR BIT OF RESEARCH DECIDED CHILE WOULD BE THE PERFECT DESTINATION. It was somewhere totally different that would be as much an experience of culture as it would be a surf mission. And so crew assembled: Kingy, Pete Gleeson, Chris

ALEX WILLIAMS

Bryan, Alex Bunting, Luke Ottoway, Todd 'Bilson' Wilson and myself.

After a long journey the town we arrived in hugged the coastline a little bit like the Gold Coast, with hotels, casinos, clubs and shops lining the foreshore. But the barren, mountain backdrop, roofless dingy houses and dirty streets quickly reminded us that we were in a developing country.

Our taxi driver brought us to a point

on the coast that we'd recognised on Kingy's map … a sick right reef setup and a left across the channel indicated that we were on the right track. Upon further inspection of the map and witnessing a bomb set unloading glassy, spitting barrels on both the left and right, we knew we were EXACTLY where we wanted to be.

On the morning of day four a 6-8ft swell was pounding the reefs. The left looked thick and mean with some incredibly wide barrels rolling through. The wind was light offshore as it had been for the past three mornings. On the beach, Kingy, Bryan and Gleeso

witnessed a mugging only 50 metres away. An American chick filming her boyfriend in the surf was stabbed in the shoulder by a junkie who attempted to run off with her tripod and camera. She screamed and within seconds the thief was run down by local boys who proceed to kick the shit out of him – heavy!

By thorough study of Kingy's maps and photos of our destined lefthander

in a local surf mag, we managed to locate and identify the spot we'd driven five hours for…and, sure enough, it was pumping!! A fresh 6-8ft swell was pounding on the reef, and powerful lefthand barrels were terminating dangerously close to exposed barnacle-covered rocks.

"Was this the right spot?" we asked each other puzzled. There was not a soul in sight, the wave looked sketchy, the sky was grey and the water a dark, eerie-looking brown colour. Moments later another solid 6ft set throttled down the reef, every wave barreling hard and spitting at the end. "This has gotta be the spot fellas," I said with a lump in my throat, "Lets hit it!" Kingy, Buntos and I timed the sketchy rock-jump and slowly made our way to the lineup. The first set came through and we each rode conservatively ahead of a fast, thick barrel. "This place has got some grunt ay!" I said to Kingy paddling out. We watched an empty one throw out a perfect cavern in front of us. "It looks like Pipe out here!" Kingy said excitedly. A few more bombs throttled past us and we were racing each other to get to the peak, this place was sick! For the next five hours we were pushing each other deeper in to the peak and becoming more familiar with the crazy launch ramp at the end.

We felt enlightened. At the start no-one knew what to expect and we were continually surprised with positive experiences. By the end of our trip we all spoke a little Spanish and we'd made plenty of new friends along the way. Most of all though, we'd seen and experienced a part of the world that we would never have seen had we not followed our instincts at the beginning. We have Kingy to thank for initiating this trip of chance that has certainly paid off.

HARDY BOOSTS A HUGE INVERT ON ONE OF THE MAIDEN
TRIPS BY INTERNATIONAL PRO'S TO EL GRINGO.

CENTRAL AMERICA

BRAVE THE DANGERS OF THE JUNGLE TO FIND SOME REAL MAYAN TREASURE

COSTA RICA
LANGUAGE.....**SPANISH**
MAIN AIRPORT.....**JUAN SANTAMARIA INTERNATIONAL AIRPORT (SJO)**
CURRENCY.....**COSTA RICAN COLON**
SWELL SEASON.....**PACIFIC YEAR ROUND, CARIBBEAN DEC-MAR**
WATER TEMP.....**27C-28C**

PANAMA
LANGUAGE.....**SPANISH**
MAIN AIRPORT.....**TOCUMEN INTERNATIONAL AIRPORT (PTY)**
CURRENCY.....**PANAMANIAN BALBOA / US DOLLAR**
SWELL SEASON.....**PACIFIC YEAR ROUND, CARIBBEAN DEC-MAR**
WATER TEMP.....**27C-28C**

NICARAGUA
LANGUAGE.....**SPANISH**
MAIN AIRPORT.....**AUGUSTO C. SANDINO INTERNATIONAL AIRPORT (MGA)**
CURRENCY.....**NICARAGUAN CORDOBA**
SWELL SEASON.....**PACIFIC YEAR ROUND, CARIBBEAN DEC-MAR**
WATER TEMP.....**27C-28C**

OUTLINE

Technically the meandering tail of North America, Central America forms part of the tropical isthmus to South America flanked by both the Pacific Ocean and the Caribbean Sea. Lush, rich and fertile, the landscape is mountainous and geologically active, with several active volcanoes grumbling away deep in the forests.

The twisty and diverse coastlines receive swell from both sides and boast every conceivable break a bodyboarder could wish for, in warm water, without the crowds of the more well-known locations. From the dream wedges and beachies of Nicaragua to the sick reefs and shories of Costa Rica and Panama, the region is a veritable hotbed of bodyboarding waves just waiting to be discovered and lapped up.

BREAKS

The multi-directional dual coastlines of the region mean there are an incredible number of epic spots to be found. These breaks are serviced by the super-consistent Pacific Ocean swells which batter the west coast, and the seasonal yet punchy east Caribbean Sea swell which gives some of the most fun waves in the whole hemisphere. Despite a boom in surf travellers over the last few decades in countries like Mexico and Costa Rica, other nations in the region are comparatively new to the game and packed full of virgin secrets to be dug up — no doubt breaking pristinely in front of some wild green jungle filled with monkeys, parrots and jaguars.

FERNANDO MUNOZ

EUNATE AGUIRRE PULLS IN TO A PANAMANIAN SHACK.

AIDAN SALMON

BLUFF, PROBABLY THE MOST FUN BODYBOARDING WAVE IN THE CARIBBEAN.

BLUFF, PANAMA

The best bodyboarding spot in the Caribbean Sea, Bluff breaks in the Bocas del Toro islands during the seasonal swell period of December to February, and can pack a real punch. A powerful, hollow shorey, Bluff has several kilometers of open beach which gives superb beachy peaks and barrels just made for the boog. When holding double overhead leashes aren't even advised, the place breaks like a mini Puerto Escondido. South west winds are offshore and feather the lips of the predominant right-hand barrels which speed down the shallow sandbank before either popping you an air section or hollowing out even further into oblivion. Bluff is on the edge of a pristine wilderness of islands, and although bodyboarding is gaining popularity, it is never crowded out and the mellow vibe is more Caribbean than mainland Central America.

LA PUNTA, PANAMA

Breaking off a small island in the Gulf of Chiriqui off Panama's west coast, La Punta is an amazing left hand reefbreak which pitches fast and hollow and is one of the easiest places to get slotted in Central America. After an easy take off the section becomes more square and funnels into a nice round pit which lets you sit tight or attack the lip and hit the eject button. Not particularly long but heavy and intense, La Punta works best on a mid tide and can handle big swell.

FERNANDO MUÑOZ

PEREZ PUNTS AT LA PUNTA, THIS PLACE IS A MISSION BUT DEFINITELY WORTH IT WITH BOWLS LIKE THESE!

CALLAHAN

SOUP BOWL, BARBADOS

Considered the best break in the Caribbean, Soup Bowl is a round, warping hollow right hander breaking over a sharp coral reef off Bathsheba on the east coast of Barbados. The bowl is thick and there are always sections to punch out of. Heavily afflicted by the E/NE trades, you have a better chance of scoring it clean early and late when the winds die a little, but even when it is onshore you can still scoop into some chunky crystal blue barrels. Watch out for the urchins on the inside, and the wrapping shutdowns when there is too much north in the swell.

IT'S NOT JUST SOUP BOWL THAT IT'S WORTH VISITING THE ISLAND FOR. ONE OF THE MANY SICK SET UPS THAT YOU CAN FIND BY SEARCHING AROUND THE COAST OF BARBADOS.

STU NORTON

COSTA RICA HAS MANY SICK SETUPS.

SALSA BRAVA, COSTA RICA

Just over the Costa Rican border from Panama sits one of the best reef breaks on the entire coast, Puerto Viejo's Salsa Brava. It can hold big east swells and breaks hollow and heavy with a late takeoff and two thick sections to negotiate. There is a left too which is shorter and arguably more intense. S/SW winds are best to groom the faces before they guillotine. Don't get caught inside at Salsa, the reef is shallow and can really sharpen its claws to teach you how to dance.

SHARPY

AIDAN SALMON ESCAPED THE UK WINTER WITH A TRIP TO CENTRAL AMERICA. THE FRUITS OF HIS MISSION BEING THIS EPIC, WEDGEY SHORE BREAK. THERE ARE PLENTY MORE OUT THERE, GO TAKE A LOOK!

WEDGE, NICARAGUA

This hollow left hand wedge is just perfect for bodyboarding. Super consistent, the waves at this secret spot never seem to go flat and are constantly groomed by offshore breezes. This is due to Lake Nicaragua just inland, which alters the atmospheric thermodynamics to make the winds blow offshore every day, grooming the lines of swell which refract off the rocks at the southern end of the beach. The takeoff fires you down the line through kegs and into oncoming sections to tweak your aerials — the ultimate playground. Works best after mid tide to almost high (when it becomes a little backwashy) and again on the drop to mid, giving almost six hours of working wedge a day. Due to the number of American standups who usually surf down the beach at other peaks it is relatively quiet in the lineup. Nicaragua is one of the last undiscovered surf regions, check google earth, the potential is insane. Living is cheap, the surf is super-consistent, the weather perfect and local food good. What more could you want?

KRIS INCH

THE WEDGE DOING ITS THING, DAY IN, DAY OUT.

CENTRAL AMERICA TRAVEL TIPS
There are a great many dangers when travelling throughout Central America including wild animals, jungle insects and nasty diseases, which are all ever-present due to the tropical climates and all the joys that brings. Make sure you get the requisite jabs and medicines you need if you are entering areas of known diseases, which can include malaria, cholera, rabies, hepatitis, typhoid, dengue fever and yellow fever. Check for outbreaks before travelling and make sure you are covered.

Most of the countries in Central America speak Spanish, so if you don't know any it is wise to learn some basic phrases to help make your trip that bit easier. Although English is spoken in some countries, it can't hurt to learn a bit of the local lingo – even if the person you are speaking to only knows broken English and you keyworded Spanish, you're at least halfway there in coming to an understanding.

Other unfortunate possibilities in Central America are crime, theft and armed attacks. Widespread poverty and social imbalance contributes more to this than anything, although gang violence in larger urban areas is not uncommon. Nor, for that matter, is the drug trade, which runs through Central America like its mountain ranges.

Many of the countries in Central America have had a volatile and violent history of social and civil unrest, and those legacies are still felt today to a degree. Having the sense to not be showy of expensive goods when out and about, keeping your bags locked, and moving on swiftly through bad neighbourhoods should improve your chances of a trouble-free trip. Oh, and travel insurance!

BOOGVIBE
Bodyboarding is big in the more recognised pockets of Central America, and the standard of riding is as solid as the waves they have here on tap. As you delve off the beaten track further into the twisty region you will find small groups of bodyboarders busting out, but it is still a growing sport. Be sure to meet the local boogers, be generous and you will be welcomed – and you never know, they may even give you a heads up to a sick secret setup somewhere in the jungle.

SHARPY

Shacked and Hijacked in Central America

By Kris Inch

WHILST BROWSING THE INTERNET ONE EVENING I CAME ACROSS SOME SHOTS OF A BEACH BREAK DOING A REASONABLE IMPRESSION OF KEIKI (EXCEPT TOTALLY MAKEABLE). AN HOUR OR SO LATER I HAD WORKED OUT THAT THE BEACH WAS LOCATED ON AN ISLAND OFF THE CARIBBEAN COAST OF PANAMA AND, AFTER

READING STATEMENTS SUCH AS: 'HOLLOW AND POWERFUL WAVES BREAKING SUPER-CLOSE TO SHORE', AND 'BETTER THAN HOSSEGOR', I KNEW I HAD TO GO TO THIS PLACE, THE ISLANDS OF BOCAS DEL TORO.

Most people that visit these islands stay in the main town on Isla Colon, aptly named Bocas Town, but I had arranged to stay at a place called Tesoro Escondido, almost five miles

away but within walking distance of all the waves. This proved to be the best decision I could have made. The islands are amazing and covered in lush jungle, teeming with incredible wildlife such as sloths, parrots and poisonous red frogs. Soon after I arrived I headed straight to a beach known as Bluff about two minutes from where I was staying, this was the beach break that I had seen photos of, and was pretty much what made me come to this part of the world..

A couple of days later the wind swung offshore and it became epic. Bluff delivered perfect 4-6 foot spitting barrels breaking about six foot from shore. It's

undoubtedly one of the heaviest breaks I've surfed. Size-for-size it's as heavy as Puerto Escondido. And it's totally uncrowded. There was a Portuguese booger who surfed it occasionally, but most of the time I had it to myself. It was ridiculous. Bluff is the best bodyboard wave on the island by far, but there are also a few sick reefs that go off and are virtually empty. Basically, Bocas Del Toro on a decent swell is bodyboard heaven, and definitely one of the best and most beautiful places I have ever been.

After two weeks of epic waves I left Bocas and travelled back to San Jose to meet my girlfriend Francesca who had

SHARPY

flown in for a few weeks before starting a new job. We had planned to do a bit of cultural sightseeing before returning to the surf. After spending a few fun days in touristy Tamarindo, we travelled north through Nicaragua and Honduras. After dark one evening we were on a bus in northern Guatemala, I was sat at the front next to the driver, and Francesca was seated further back as these were the only available seats when we got on. Suddenly there was shouting from further back on the bus, at first I thought nothing of it as the locals often seem to be shouting about something or other.

When the shouting continued I turned around to see what was going on and was greeted by the sight of a gun inches from my face. For the next 15 minutes the bus was held at gunpoint by a gang of five men who proceeded to rob and body search everyone. You never know how you would react in a situation like this until it happens, and I thought I would have been shitting myself, but surprisingly I wasn't really scared – just seriously pissed off that I was having all my shit stolen. Once the thieving pricks were done, they made the driver stop and got off the bus shooting into the air

as they went.

And so, with no passport, money or ID there was no option but to come home. The following week was spent going to and from the British Embassy in scummy Guatemala City to get emergency passports, and then flying home for a mere $1500 – which my insurance company took great pleasure in telling me they wouldn't cover me for.

With the

exception of one major gun-related setback, Central America was a genuinely sick trip, and definitely proved itself to me as the most underrated bodyboarding destination. Even with spiders and gunpoint robbery: I'll be going back for sure.

SHARPY

MEXICO

SOME OF THE MOST CONSISTENT AND HEAVIEST BEACHBREAKS ON EARTH

COSTA RICA
LANGUAGE.....**SPANISH**
MAIN AIRPORT.....**MEXICO CITY**
INTERNATIONAL AIRPORT (MEX)
CURRENCY.....**MEXICAN PESO**
SWELL SEASON.....**PACIFIC YEAR**
ROUND, CARIBBEAN DEC-MAR
WATER TEMP.....**24C-31C**

ALAN VAN GYSEN

OUTLINE

Mexico sits south of the United States in an area slightly less than three times the size of Texas. Its geography and climate vary greatly, from a dry, arid and rugged north to a lush, tropical and jungle-covered south. Featuring deserts, plains, lakes, plateaus, gorges, canyons, mountains and volcanoes, its terrain is as varied as its natural hazards, which include tsunamis,

volcanoes, earthquakes and hurricanes.

Mexico has more than 9,300km of coastline, and it is no wonder that with much of the south west-facing stretch battered by unhinged Pacific swells — welcomed in full by an offshore deepwater trench — its beachies are aptly described as 'Hossegor on steroids'. If you can get through the wet heat and mosquitoes without being held up by at gunpoint, the fabled Mexican beachies are a humbling destination.

BREAKS

It isn't all just about leash-straightening beachies in Mexico, it also has an abundance of points, rivermouths and reefs which can all fire on spec, and routinely do. While each year from April to October boogers flock to the big barrels of Puerto Escondido to test their mettle, the potential for uncrowded perfection up and down the Mex coast is unbounded. With such a high swell consistency and so many breaks explorable off the coastal lifeline of Highway 200, it is wide open to the more hardcore travellers who aren't afraid of onshore hold-ups and offshore hold-downs.

"Mexico is my favourite place to go on the world tour, such a nice place with a really fun atmosphere. It's a great place to go on holiday and definitely one of the best spots in the world to go bodyboarding." - Jake Stone

ALAN VAN GYSEN

PASQUALES

If there is any other beachbreak able to compete with the heaviness and size of Puerto Escondido, this is it. Pasquales can unload massive unpredictable beasts, which even if you make out of, still scare you half to death. The hell sneaker sets and random closeout sections which shift around don't help matters, and combine that with moving channels, shallow sandbars and big currents, you have a melting pot of doubt, even on a medium day. There is not much to do in the village here, so you really only come to surf the dark freight trains off the black sand beach...which give you both a major shot of adrenaline and a horrible knot in your stomach all at once. These bombs keep you up at night: if the sound of a distant booming set imploding on the sandbank doesn't, what it does in your mind as you try to sleep surely will. You can't help but feel Pasquales considers every successful barrel you make as a personal insult, and it's only a matter of time before it takes its sinister revenge. It works best on NE wind and west to south swell.

PASQUALES LOOKING SUPER FUN.

LEE KELLY

"Puerto Escondido is one of the best beachbreaks on earth, so consistent and so good for bodyboarding! It depends on the banks but you should find some big barrels and massive ramps. During the IBA contest in 2011, I saw one of the best waves I have ever seen!" - Amaury Lavernhe

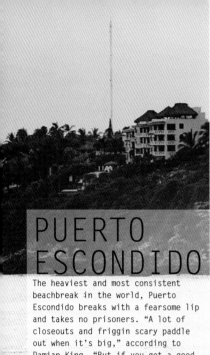

PUERTO ESCONDIDO

The heaviest and most consistent beachbreak in the world, Puerto Escondido breaks with a fearsome lip and takes no prisoners. "A lot of closeouts and friggin scary paddle out when it's big," according to Damian King, "But if you get a good one you'll know all about it!" Detonating right and left with a strong rip, Puerto can hold massive swell and breaks with a brutal power with no channels, often closing out. It is a given that at some point in your session at Puerto you will get a flogging. Its openness to raw south swells from May to October means waves can increase in size in a session very quickly, and assault the sandbanks at Puerto; comparable to a reef but less predictable. A favourite for giant-barrel hunters, to claim a quadruple overhead keg at Puerto makes all the pummeling wipeouts almost worth it. Rise at dawn to get the offshore NE wind as it nearly always turns onshore by 11am. It breaks throughout the tides and is rarely flat, although two- or three-week flat spells are common in January. It can get crowded when small to medium size, but after it starts to get big the crowds thin out pretty damn quickly — the paddle out goes from tough to almost impossible.

BOOGVIBE

Bodyboarding is big in Mexico and riders from all over the world come to Puerto Escondido each year to try their luck in front of the crowds of bloodthirsty photographers, mingling with a solid local bodyboarding community which has developed and flourished over the years. In addition to the media circus, and unlike some lesser-known places in Central America, there are bodyboard shops here too, so replacing the kit you will inevitably snap is right at hand.

MEXICO TRAVEL TIPS

Millions of travellers visit Mexico every year, but it has to be said Mexico has more than its fair share of dangers, in part due to the ongoing war on the vicious drug and gun cartels that control the flow of drug trafficking north into the US. Most of this activity happens near the US border, expecially around the cities of Tijuana near California and Ciudad Juarez over the border from Texas, although many states also experience drug related violence. As of the end of 2011, the state of Oaxaca, in which Puerto Escondido is located is relatively peaceful. The key is to do your research before you leave and stay out of areas where the rule of law is flimsy to say the least. Your country's Foreign Office or State Department's website is a useful first port of call for current warnings.

Although most Mexicans you'll meet will be kind and pleased to meet you, muggings, pickpocketing and crime are all too common in built-up and poverty-stricken areas, so always keep your bags close to hand and your valuables and wallet hidden. Be wary of dodgy bystanders hanging around

a little close for comfort and watch out for police officers attempting to fine or arrest you for no particular reason, they may well not be cops at all.

Mexico is the most populous Spanish-speaking country in the world (way more than double that of Spain), so learn the basics and photocopy the language pages of a guide book to stuff in your pocket when out and about, your gringo attempt at rolling your R's could get you a decent haggle.

When taking money out of cash machines make sure you do so in daylight, and put your money away immediately before turning to leave. It is also worth separating your cash and stashing some elsewhere in your gear so if you do have your wallet stolen you aren't penniless. When you are drawing out money, watch out for the 200 peso note which will inevitably come your way; no-one seems to have any change in Mexico and you won't be flavour of the month trying to buy something small with it. Head to a big store to break it up and get as much change and small denomination notes as you can for food,

cab fares and bits.

Be sure to check out traditional Mexican food – it is extremely cheap and is sure to give you a newfound respect for flavour. However, watch out for the water, you will need to drink a lot of it to replenish lost fluids due to the heat in Mexico, but make sure it is distilled or from a sealed bottled or you will find yourself getting pretty sick pretty quickly. That goes for washing fruit and vegetables too, peel them if possible.

Despite your best efforts you will almost certainly still be struck by a bug, so bring anti-diarrhoea tablets and rehydration salts so you are not land-bound for a minute more than you have to be. There is little worse than shitting through the eye of a needle in preying swarms of mozzies whilst perfect 3-5ft A-frames are peeling through uncrowded out front.

BRAZIL
PURE UNHINGED BODYBOARDING HEDONISM

COSTA RICA
LANGUAGE.....**PORTUGUESE**
MAIN AIRPORT.....**RIO DE JANEIRO GALEAO ANTONIO CARLOS JOBIM INTERNATIONAL AIRPORT (GIG)**
CURRENCY.....**BRAZILIAN REAL**
SWELL SEASON.....**APR-OCT**
WATER TEMP.....**21C-28C**

OUTLINE

Brazil is the biggest country in South America and fifth largest country in the world, both by area and population. It features the greatest biological diversity in the world, and is home to the Amazon River, the biggest in the world (in terms of volume) and the Amazon rainforest, the largest tropical forest

SPECKER / IBA

TOP BRAZILIAN IBA COMPETITOR MAGNO OLIVEIRA BUSTS A BACKFLIP.

in the world. It also has a coastline spanning more than 4,650 miles – with the waves to match.

One of the more underrated countries for waves, southern Brazil gets a ridiculous amount of south Antarctic swellsfrom April to October, which switch on hundreds of top spots along the south-facing coastline near Rio de Janeiro. Huge wedges, pounding shorebreaks and ledging reefs are the go, projecting hardened Brazilian groms on a steep learning curve.

BREAKS

While the more crowded south-facing coastline gets battered with the big S/SE Antarctic swell in the Brazilian winter, the huge north east region catches the northerly Atlantic swells in the summer. This fires up the numerous beaches, reefs and points littering the vast coastline, and includes the offshore island of Fernando de Noronha, which is extremely consistent and whose offshore deepwater trench makes for some very powerful spots. Due to the shape and length of the Brazilian coastline and its unimpeded exposure to swells from different directions, Brazil rarely goes flat and there are so many breaks yet to be discovered it has some serious potential.

BOOGVIBE

Bodyboarding in Brazil is massive, with huge support for the sport and its riders on the beach and in the media. The well known spots all have frothing packs of spongers shredding, and many of Brazil's underground riders could go on to do very well on the IBA world tour if they were to ever get funding. Brazilians are known for their 'charge-hard' attitude to tackling heavy waves, epitomised by national hero and six-time world champion Guilherme Tamega. His unique style and powerful approach to his riding has set the benchmark for Brazilian riders, and there are many hot on his heels despite ripping in obscurity.

"Brazil for me is all about having FUN.. the people are friendly, the food is cheap, ladies are amazing and the waves are a lot better than what you think. Wedgy beachbreaks in every corner and slabbing reef breaks off every headland. If you want a holiday where all you do is surf all day, eat cheap food and hook up with girls who in your own country won't even look at you, then this is the place! If you're a single man you owe yourself a trip to Brazil...NOW!" - Matt Lackey

"My favourite spots in Brazil are the reef breaks located in the state of Espirito Santo which is one hour north of Rio by plane. Rio de janeiro is the most consistent place in Brazil, nearly every week there's a good south swell hits it. The best waves are Itacoatiara, sao Conrado, Joaquina, Copacabana and many more." - Magno Oliveira

SHOREBREAK

Despite its name, Shorebreak is totally sick right hand slab which breaks off the right end of the headland at Copacabana Beach next to a military base and looks like a tanned cousin of Shark Island. Over 3-4ft the place gets very very heavy and breaks over a shallow ledge, much like the Island. Works well on S/SW swell, and N/NW winds. It is square, after the drop you need every inch of your rail to fight the warp and hope to come out with the spit - this place is sponge heaven.

BEN DeCAMP

ITACOATIARA

Arguably the best beachbreak in Brazil,
Itacoatiara is around an hour up the coast
from Rio on the east side of the bay entrance.
Fully south-facing, it's home to fast,
hollow, powerfully short waves which break
extremely heavily on the banks, making it
almost exclusively a bodyboard wave. Offshore
on a northerly wind, it handles massive swell
and breaks similarly to the heavier spots
in Mexico. One of the hidden dangers here is
being able to concentrate on the approaching
sets as almost every bikini-clad girl that
visits the beach is straight out of a Reef
calendar, it is bordering on the ridiculous.

"This is Copacabana 'Posto 5'. It's the Puerto Escondido of Brazil on a solid south east swell with south winds head here. There is one area of the beach that the locals call "Posto 5" that delivers romping peaks just meters from the beach. You will be met with 100's of talented bodyboarders that live in the nearby favelas who are all super friendly." - Matt Lackey

BRAZIL TRAVEL TIPS

The story is the same in many of the Central and South American countries when it comes to travelling around – be sensible, take basic

precautions when exploring and read up on which areas to avoid, especially in favela-flanked cities like Rio de Janeiro. Despite its beautiful beaches, tourism and modern hotel-clad strips, a few blocks back is a different world of poverty, crime and violence. The drug gangs of the slums are armed with enough hardware to make flak jackets and bullet-proof vests useless, and even young kids are versed well in how to rob with guns. You can of course improve your chances of not getting into trouble by avoiding jaunts into Rio's favelas, especially at night. It is worth hiding your valuables anyway, stash your day money away and carry a fake second wallet (full of unwanted business cards, a few bucks and a couple of old bank cards which don't work anymore). Maintain low key and you should be fine, but if you do get held up (it happens), give it up right away and hope they're in a rush.

Some of the more urban surf spots will no doubt have a hardcore local crew of guys who will charge and flagrantly ignore conventional lineup etiquette. Roll with it – some of them may well be from the favelas where law and order doesn't exactly feature prominently, so it's safe to say surf manners won't much either. It isn't worth the aggro to get involved with some of these guys so suck it up, sit back and let them rule the roost if things turn ugly, you'll get your share of waves eventually. (And if not there are a million other spots nearby, should you outstay your welcome).

The partying in Brazil is mental, the girls are ridiculously beautiful and all rock the G-string as

standard attire. Nightlife is buzzing and never stops; clubs, parties, street gatherings, the vibe is always upbeat and friendly, and despite comparative poverty, they party like millionaires. If you arrive during carnival in February or March (dates vary), you will have the time of your life. You can even take part in the parade by buying a costume and joining a samba school. Check out www.rio-carnival.net for info.

Although wealthy Brazilians will probably know English to a good standard, most of the less affluent population won't, so it's worth getting a Portuguese language book to brush up on for the flight. Rio's public transport system is excellent with many cheap ways of getting about; although traffic is at best a complete nightmare, so if you do fancy renting a vehicle, expect carnage.

Brazilian food is delicious, and you will fall in love with many traditional dishes from region to region, so (as with anywhere) get involved with the local food scene and forget western food outlets – you won't regret it.

SHOCK

```
A sick, insanely slabbing right hand reef
which breaks off the west end of Itacoatiara
Beach, about 10km east of Rio, and delivers
short, fast, warping pits which could almost
pass as a makeable Cyclops. It is a badass
slab which is extremely heavy and isn't
afraid of dishing out some rough justice.
Works best on south swell and north winds.
If you do mis-time and get destroyed on the
reef at least you have the beach girls of
Itacoatiara to give you the kiss of life.
```

LEME

One of the heaviest wedges ridden, Leme does a
passable impression of Newport Wedge in California,
and can handle some serious chunks. Huge south swells
roll up the rocky cliff face on the northeastern end
of Copacabana Beach before refracting back into a peak
which can hold 12ft plus, even bigger when the factors
all line up perfectly. An insanely round barrel and
massive boost section are on offer (if you have balls
like watermelons), although it can be inconsistent.
It works best on a NW wind but is pretty protected
from the easterlies if that's all you have. The local
bodyboard crew shred the wedge to pieces when it's on,
and seemingly don't have fear — probably as a result
of some of them growing up in the local favelas.

RESOURCES

USEFUL WEBSITES

wannasurf.com
Getting a little dated these days but has tons of useful user generated info and photos on surf spots around the world.

magicseaweed.com
The first stop for free swell forecasts, photos and info on most of the major spots around the globe. Useful historical swell data will help you judge the best time to go to a particular spot.

windguru.cz
A pure swell forecast site. You have to upgrade to a Pro account to get the full service.

surfline.com
Big US-based website with surfcams and surf forecasts. The basic info is free but you need to upgrade to get more detailed info and access to some surfcams.

ibaworldtour.com
The governing body of world bodyboarding. Info, videos and webcasts featuring the pro tour.

lonelyplanet.com
Tons of useful free online travel info on dozens of destinations. There's also a useful forum called Thorn Tree on which you can post questions and search for info on countries and destinations from other users.

fluidzone.com
Australian site with a good forum, plus surf forecasts for Australian spots, galleries, videos and news.

riptidemag.com.au
Good source of news from the iconic Aussie mag's online resource.

movementmag.com
Inspirational photos, mostly from Australia.

vert-mag.com
This Portuguese site isn't in English, but there are plenty of galleries to get you stocked.

sixty40.co.za
South African mag with a good source of news. The travel forum is a great source of information and tips from fellow bodyboarding travellers.

thesurfdirectory.co.uk
Useful source of info on spots and accommodation in the UK and Ireland.

threesixtymag.co.uk
UK site with tons of news and info.

flickr.com
A big general photo sharing and social networking site. Worth searching for photos of spots you're planning to visit for inspiration.

couchsurfing.org
Networking site putting travellers in contact with like-minded travellers who provide a free bed to sleep in for a few days.

onebag.com
Website offering exhaustive detail on the art and science of travelling light.

moneysavingexpert.com
Good source of information on how to get cheap flights and save heaps on everything from budget airline fees to foreign exchange.

HEALTH INFORMATION

Your doctor will be able to advise you on which vaccinations are required for your destination, but for your own research, check these sites:

traveldoctor.co.uk
Really useful, well laid out site stuffed with information on vaccinations, health tips, etc.

mdtravelhealth.com
Good general informormation and advice.

travelclinic.com.au
Chain of Australian clinics offering vaccinations.

GOVERNMENT INFORMATION

A first port of call for general information on travelling abroad (checking visa requirements and so on) is your own government, especially if you are journeying to obscure or potentially unstable parts of the world. Make sure your passport is current and has at least six months to go before it expires, many countries will refuse entry if it is not. Here are some links:

UNITED KINGDOM
fco.gov.uk — Foreign and Colonial Office.
www.nhs.uk — National Health Service
fitfortravel.nhs.uk — NHS information for travellers.

UNITED STATES
travel.state.gov — State Department
cdc.gov — Centers for Disease Control and Prevention

AUSTRALIA
smartraveller.gov.au — The Australian Government's travel advisory and consular information service. You can also register your personal and travel details here.

NEW ZEALAND
safetravel.govt.nz — official source of advice for New Zealanders

SOUTH AFRICA
dfa.gov.za — Department for International Relations.

IRELAND
dfa.ie — Department for Foreign Affairs
tmb.ie — Tropical Medicine Bureau

WORDLWIDE
who.int — The UN's World Health Organization provides information on worldwide health matters. The first port of call for infomation on scary outbreaks of infectious diseases.

RESOURCES

SHOPS

Any travelling bodyboarder needs to make sure that they will be on the right equipment for their destination. Make sure that you speak to a bodyboard store that has the knowledge to get you on the correct ride for your height, weight, riding style and the destinations and water temperature that you will be using the gear in. These bodyboarder-run businesses have supported us in producing this book, so check them out first.

bodyboarders.com.au

bodyboarders.com.au is the home of leading Australian bodyboard shop chain Bodyboarders Surf Company. They have stores in Sydney, on the Gold Coast and are also one of the leading online stores. From fins, to wetties, to leash plugs, they will have the right kit and the experience to match you up with it.

ebodyboarding.com

Long time pro bodyboarder Jay Reale, a guy that has seen and done it all, and certainly one of the best bodyboarding knowledges in the world, has one of the best online stores in the US, with all the kit to have you ripping in any water temperature and some of the best available, full stop.

bodyboardking.com.au

One of the leading Australian stores, owned by pro bodyboarder Toby Player, BodyboardKing have all the leading brands, a world beating team of riders and they ship worldwide. Check them out for all the cutting edge equipment.

bodyboard-depot.com

The UK based bodyboard store run by Rob Barber and his team. They have a solid range of boards, fins, clothing and accessories and plenty of travel knowledge for you to tap in to. Boards in the UK are some of the cheapest that they are in the world, so always worth checking them out. They've also got a Newquay based store.

HOLIDAYS/VACATIONS

surftravel.com.au

The Surf Travel Company is a name that is synonymous with international surf travel and adventure and has been since it pioneered the fledgling industry 20 years ago. Every bodyboarder that has ever been on a trip to Indo, the Maldives, PNG, the Pacific or any far flung surfing destination owes a small legacy to STC, because without the foresight and dedication to the travelling surfer, such opportunities would remain only for the hardcore explorer. The Surf Travel Company now offer dedicated bodyboarding packages, check them out.

bodyboard-holidays.com

Bodyboard coaching holidays for all ages and abilities to international destinations including; Indonesia, Morocco, Lanzarote, Gran Canaria, Costa Rica, Ireland and the UK. Rob Barber and his team of qualified, experienced coaches help you to improve your riding, guide you to the best waves that the area has to offer, giving you peace of mind but at the same time increase the fun. They make sure that you're in the right place, at the right time and they use beach work and video analysis to help you improve your riding fast!

balibodyboarding.com

With 10 years of travel experience in Indonesia, Bali Bodyboarding offer comprehensive surf guiding, coaching and holiday packages throughout the archipelago for all ability levels. If you're after a wave riding adventure of a lifetime, Indonesia is the place and Bali Bodyboarding will make it happen for you.

BODYBOARDING SCHOOLS

bodyboard-school.com

Incredibly there appears to be only one dedicated bodyboarding school in the English speaking world! Rob Barber's bodyboarding school is based in Newquay, Cornwall, England, and also runs organised trips to Indo, Morocco and the Canary Islands.

bodyboardhouse.com

Based in southwest France, runs lessons as well as trips abroad. Appears to be only French speaking.

surfingaustralia.com

Runs bodyboard coaching clinics.

In Portugal there is novaonda.com based in Carcavelos, and escolasbbpeniche.web in Peniche.

FURTHER READING

We deliberately didn't provide detailed maps and guidance to every surf break in each region, that wasn't the intention of this book. There's a ton of surf guides that do this, here are the best, although none of them are aimed at bodyboarders:

Stormrider Guides by Low Pressure Publishing. The original surf guides started with Europe, expanded to the world and now has guides covering different surfing regions, including Indo and Central America . On their website lowpressure.co.uk, you can download ebooks and there's a useful wavefinder tool, as well an app.

Wavefinder guides are little pocket guides that fit in the palm of your hand and basically list virtually every spot. There's a guide for the USA, including Hawaii, as well as Mexico, the UK and Ireland, Australia, Indo and Central America. wave-finder.com

Footprint guides publish surf guides (some of which are out of print but may still be available on amazon second hand) to The UK and Ireland, Europe and the world. footprinttravelguides.com

Finally, a couple of books by the publishers of this tome which will come in handy: The Threesixty Bodyboard Manual is a low cost guide to improving your bodyboarding and The Complete Guide to Surf Fitness will help you get in shape for your travels. Free worldwide shipping is available from orcashop.co.uk, or you can order them from amazon.

FoundBoards

bodyboard-holidays

YOUR BODYBOARDING TRIP OF A LIFETIME STARTS HERE...
www.Bodyboard-Holidays.com

INTERNATIONAL BODYBOARD COACHING HOLIDAYS FOR ALL AGES AND ABILITIES

DESTINATIONS INCLUDE:

MOROCCO   GRAN CANARIA   COSTA RICA   LANZAROTE   INDONESIA

Check out our Bodyboard Shop: www.Bodyboard-Depot.com   Bodyboard School: www.Bodyboard-School.com

facebook.com/bodyboard-depot

INDEX

ABOUT THE AUTHORS

OWEN PYE

Freelance journalist and bodyboarder Owen Pye was born in Cornwall, England, and holds UK and US citizenship. An honours degree graduate from UWIC, he has travelled extensively and holds a Masters in International Journalism from UCF. He has worked as an entertainment reporter for New York Magazine in Manhattan, international news reporter for The Associated Press out of its Sydney bureau, and local reporter for The West Briton newspaper in the UK.

Owen is a staff writer for ThreeSixty Bodyboard Magazine and Carve Surfing Magazine, and also regularly contributes for Japan Airlines' Skyward Magazine. Articles he has written for the AP have appeared for such publications as The New York Times, The LA Times, The Guardian and The Washington Post.

Owen has worked as a specialist in the bodyboard industry for more years than he cares to remember and has surfed on five continents, uncovered new waves on boat trips to the distant fringes of Pacific islands, and seen more of Australia than a Qantas pilot. He is very happy to have a career that combines three of his passions - writing, photography and travel.

ROB BARBER PHOTOGRAPHED BY MIKE SEARLE IN MOROCCO IN 2010.

ROB BARBER

Rob Barber is the editor of ThreeSixty, the most respected bodyboard magazine in Europe. He has been at the very core of British bodyboarding for as many years as most can remember; learning at Fistral Beach in 1987 and is still on every swell at Tolcarne Wedge. Rob opened his first school 'Rob Barber's Bodyboarding School' when he was 18 years old; two years later he launched the world's first bodyboard coaching holidays company and this was followed by a surf school, a coasteer school and more recently a bodyboard shop, The Bodyboard-Depot. In his sixteen years of coaching, Rob has taught thousands the ways of the boogie, from first time beginners to members of the national team.

Travel and bodyboarding exploration have been a focal point of Rob's life; he constantly travels, working on his bodyboard holidays business, for magazine-related work and to generally hunt good waves. His favourite place to score waves is Indo, but he has enjoyed waves first hand at 80% of the destinations detailed in this book.

Rob has enjoyed a successful competitive career representing Britain and England numerous times and winning more than 25 events. He finished 1995 as the highest ranked European in the world professional ratings after placing highly in the World Championships at Pipeline in Hawaii.

MIKE SEARLE

Mike Searle was first bitten by the bodyboarding bug in the late '80s, when he was living in landlocked London. Moving to Cornwall in 1991, he founded ThreeSixty bodyboard magazine, and set about teaching himself the art of surf and bodyboard photography from scratch. Since those early days he has had hundreds of photos published in publications all over the world, included ThreeSixty, Carve, The Guardian, The Sunday Times, Riptide and ASL. He was editor of ThreeSixty until the early 2000s and has travelled to the North Shore, France, Mexico, California, Morocco and the Canary Islands. His personal work can found at mikesearlephotography.co.uk